999

999

There Is Something Wrong with the System

MICHAEL ROSE

To order additional copies of this book, contact:
Xlibris
800-056-3182
www.Xlibrispublishing.co.uk
Orders@Xlibrispublishing.co.uk
789348

People are being treated badly by the nhs
healthcare system and social care industry

This book is dedicated to the survivors and the victims. When a loved one has passed away before their time, they become a number and a statistic in the national records. Everyone has a story about their life journey and there are far too many tragic stories, which have never been told and must not be forgotten.

CONTENTS

FOREWORD

When you know that something is wrong you have two choices, you can stay silent or you can speak out and take action. Hospital patients and care home residents are being abused and neglected every day and this is being covered up by the people who are controlling the agenda.

There are many dedicated staff members and professionals working in the NHS and they are trying to help people, but unfortunately many thousands of UK citizens have been mistreated by the healthcare service, mental health service, and the social care service. The facts and evidence contained in the chapters, prove that this is happening on a regular basis and there is far too much unnecessary suffering. There are a lot of doctors, nurses, and GPs who are guilty of ignorance and some of the events and details in the book are from my own personal experiences. I have seen what happens when mistakes are made and we need to ask the hospital managers and westminster politicians some important questions. Why are vulnerable individuals being abandoned by the healthcare service, mental health service, and the social care service? When you are trapped inside a failing system with a sick family member, you have to fight against the system to protect your loved one and this is unacceptable. The time has come for people to speak out and change the system and the time has come for people to take control of their medical treatment and make sure that they are taking safe medicines, instead of poisonous harmful chemicals. Human beings must be treated fairly with dignity, compassion, and respect.

1

BROKEN SYSTEM

Civil servants and business politicians are investing more than £20 billion into healthcare and social care. Unfortunately this will not fix our broken system and who actually runs the NHS and social care? The managers and chief executives are like ghosts in a machine. You can see the machine, but you can't see the ghosts because they are invisible. Hospitals are extremely busy and there is too much chaos and confusion. Everyone is in a hurry and most people appear to be lost, while they are trying to follow the signs and directions. Healthcare managers and private companies are taking control of the system. Putting an X on an election ballot paper will do absolutely nothing to change or fix this failing system because the politicians are not in control of the NHS and social care. Most people like to think that hospitals are highly efficient and organised, but after you have seen what happens in the hospital wards, you begin to realize that this is an illusion and the UK general public are not supposed to know the real truth about the incidents, which are happening behind closed doors. The national health service was created in 1948 to provide "good quality hospital care", but in reality all of the "advertising images" on display inside local hospitals and residential care homes are based upon a "false reality".

When you are in a vulnerable condition and in need of help, your rights can be easily abused by the system and the people who are carrying out the agenda, instead of following the patient care plan. Hospital doctors, nurses, psychiatrists, and mental health staff are supposed to care for their patients when they need attention and assistance, but in reality they don't have enough time to give people the care that they need because they are far too busy following NHS procedure. Individuals who need help are being treated like "numbers on a white board", which is by the side of the hospital bed. The system has taken control of healthcare and social care, the needs of sick patients are being ignored and the agenda has been given priority. The consultant doctors, nurses, psychiatrists, mental health nurses, clinicians, care workers, and the GPs are neglecting people and they are not providing proper care. It sounds like a conspiracy theory, but in reality it is a careless and robotic system, which has been created by managers, politicians, and commercial business executives and this is the "healthcare system", which is supposed to look after us when we are sick.

The doctors and the nurses will try to do their best for their patients, but in reality they cannot give proper quality care because the system is being controlled by the managers and money has become the main priority within the healthcare system. The healthcare service and the social care service are not based upon care and therapy and the family members will find out the painful truth when a loved one has passed away prematurely before their time. The system has become careless and calculating and the health and safety of vulnerable individuals is being put at risk inside hospitals, mental health wards, psychiatric wards, residential care homes, and specialist care homes for dementia and disability patients. Thousands of UK citizens are in danger and there are too many unnecessary accidents and medical errors, which are happening every day.

UK hospitals are full of problems and doctors and nurses are under pressure. There is a lack of resources and a shortage of good doctors and good nurses. The managers and the chief executives are making a lot of money, while thousands of patients are suffering because they are receiving poor quality healthcare. The higher managers are controlling "the system" and the doctors and the nurses are just the workers who carry out "the plan". There is a lot of exaggeration in the media about how wonderful the NHS is and the individuals who have received good quality healthcare are the lucky ones. Old people in hospitals and people with mental health issues and disabilities are receiving poor quality healthcare and harmful prescription drugs. Thousands of patients and residents in care homes and nursing homes are also suffering in silence due to the lack of care and this is happening on a daily basis within the private care industry.

To become a good business manager you need to be a control expert and most managers are only concerned with time and money. How long will it take and how much will it cost? This is ok if you are a restaurant manager. This is not ok if you are managing a hospital full of sick people or a care home full of old people. The hospital managers spend too much time dealing with private companies and company executives and they are ignoring the problems inside local hospitals. Elderly patients, mental health patients, patients with learning difficulties, and disabled patients are suffering because of incompetence and this is happening on a regular basis. This is the real cost of corruption and greed. The elderly who are frail and the young who are vulnerable are being failed and ignored by the healthcare system and sick patients are "being used" as a financial resource in order to feed a greedy and corrupt global pharmaceutical drug market. Large private companies are making billions of pounds out of the suffering of innocent people and global drug companies have got too much power.

When you are inside a hospital you will see all of the advanced technology, which is inside the wards and treatment rooms. Unfortunately there is a lack of common sense and intuition. The elderly are suffering due to a lack of proper care and poor quality medical treatment and this is the reality inside many local hospitals. When you go into a hospital for the first time you may notice a strange smell and after a while your senses begin to remember the scent. When you have become familiar with the scent you realize what is causing the smell. It is everywhere and most of the medical staff have got the scent on their uniforms and it is an unpleasant strong smell, which fills the air and this is unhealthy for patients because there is a lack of fresh air and most hospitals have poor ventilation with no air circulation. The scent contains toxic cleaning fluid and human waste, it is nauseating and eventually you realize what is causing the smell. Billions of pounds have been invested into healthcare, so why do the hospitals smell horrible? There is a culture of neglect within the national health service and you cannot trust in the system because the NHS is carrying out treatments, which are not in the individual's best interest.

People in hospital wards, mental health wards, and psychiatric wards are not receiving the care and attention that they need. Young people with mental health problems and young people with disabilities and learning difficulties are being abused and abandoned by the system. There is a nationwide shortage of doctors, nurses, medical staff, mental health staff, and psychiatric staff. There is also a lack of night time care across the UK and there are many elderly patients and young patients with disabilities and mental health conditions who have lost their lives because there is a total lack of proper supervision during the night time. There are questions, which need answers from the NHS managers and the politicians. When a person is admitted into hospital with a problem they will need urgent attention and medical treatment and millions of pounds have been spent on training doctors, nurses, and healthcare professionals and you don't need to be an expert to see the obvious when someone is critically ill. There are many thousands of UK pensioners inside local hospital wards, social care homes, and nursing homes who are not being looked after and they are being neglected by healthcare professionals, medical staff, and care workers. Old people are being forced to wait for long periods of time, while they are deteriorating and they are not receiving any help or assistance.

The basic quality of care inside UK hospitals is not acceptable and there are departments and wards, which are not safe for people who are seriously ill and there is a total lack of proper safeguarding. Inside my local hospital there is a unit, which is called the acute medical ward and the ward is full of very sick people. The patients are supposed to be assessed and checked and then they are taken to the ward where they will receive the correct medical treatment, but in reality time is being wasted and people are being ignored. As the clock ticks the health of the individual will continue to deteriorate. Inside these acute wards, people are left unchecked for more than two hours during the night time when they are critically ill and there is a lack of care. The acute medical ward has become like a human processing centre and the doctors and the nurses behave like robots standing around in small groups in front of computer screens, talking and having meaningless discussions about "procedure and protocol". There is too much talking and not enough care and there are old people inside small brown coloured rooms with no fresh air or sunlight and they are being neglected by the doctors and the nurses. Vulnerable individuals are being left alone at night and the hospitals are failing to provide any safeguarding inside the wards during the night time. Healthcare professionals are not fulfilling their duty of care and the system is in a state of crisis.

When you walk in through the entrance of a hospital, you will see a lot of people inside the tiny corridors and most of them are suffering due to unnecessary stress because of the lack of hospital resources. After a while you begin to notice the barriers within the system. The national health service is full of obstacles and pointless rules and the sick person's chances of survival will depend upon how much time is wasted and good luck or bad luck. "Modern healthcare" is based on a "priority system" and it does not matter if you happen to have a serious disease. If you have a life threatening disease, which is at the bottom of the priority list, you will receive poor quality care and poor treatment from medical staff who have not been trained properly and you will have to wait for long periods of time, while you are suffering because you are a "low priority" and this is unacceptable. The people who are running the healthcare service are carrying out their agenda and there is a lack of compassion within the NHS. There are diseases like tuberculosis, hepatitis, and diabetes and the doctors are ignoring these diseases. There is no money or funding available for research to find a cure for these conditions and the number of tuberculosis (TB) cases in the UK have started to rise due to the increasing migration and movement of people. TB is a complicated condition with many different kinds of bacteria. There are several types of TB infection and there is still a lot of ignorance about this particular disease within the medical establishment.

The NHS is ignoring third world epidemics and there is a lack of funding and research into "third world diseases". It should not matter where your illness comes from because everyone deserves fair treatment and it is time to help UK citizens who are suffering with curable conditions. We are giving millions in aid to foreign countries and some diseases including cancer are being given priority over respiratory conditions including tuberculosis, pneumonia, influenza, and asthma, which are also life threatening. The higher managers and chief executives who run the NHS are not in the front line of healthcare because they are too busy having endless business meetings inside expensive luxury offices and they are wasting time talking about their agendas and reaching their targets. There is a lot of fear and blame within the management culture in the government and there is too much aggression and intimidation happening behind closed doors, there is also a culture of secrecy within the national health service and the managers and the executives will do everything they can to stop the truth from coming out when they have made an error of judgement. There are hundreds of thousands of elderly hospital patients who have passed away before their time due to medical negligence and human error and the truth is still coming out, while the higher managers, chief executives, healthcare professionals, and the business politicians are trying to hide the failure of the duty of care, which is happening on a daily basis.

The healthcare service is taking away the freedom of patients and the staff numbers are too low. The staff are not able to give people good quality care and there are many flaws and issues within the design of the system. There is a big problem with technology and computer software because computers are creating the structure within the system. Unfortunately they don't have any feelings or compassion. They are good at storing data and processing information, but they can't tell if a person is in pain. The data systems in hospitals are always having problems and faults, there is too much reliance on technology and there is a lack of care in the hospital wards. The duty of care is not being fulfilled by healthcare professionals and medical staff and if the individual's care needs come into conflict with any of the rules and regulations, the medical staff are motivated by fear and they are forced to carry out NHS procedure, instead of putting the needs of the patient first. This is another reason why the system is broken. If the doctor cannot assess the individual's care needs, they will not be able to provide the correct treatment. The doctors are guilty of a lack of awareness regarding the care of the elderly and "end of life" care.

There is independent evidence of widespread neglect taking place everyday inside local hospitals across the UK. The diagnosis and treatment of the individual takes too long to happen or it doesn't happen at all because there are hundreds of other sick patients who are "waiting in the hospital queue". There aren't enough medical staff and there is a massive shortage of experienced doctors and intelligent nurses. All of the different medical departments are completely disconnected from each other due to a complete lack of communication and cooperation between the different units. If you are in pain, you will have to wait for the system and the system is too slow. There are delays and mistakes happening on a daily basis and this is having a bad effect on the health of the elderly population, there is too much unnecessary suffering and there are problems, which are not being dealt with. Most of the problems can be fixed and sorted out by using creative thinking and new investment. The managers and the government have become obsessed with reaching targets and there is a lack of care inside local hospitals. Human beings must be given priority over profit and politics and it is time for change. There are many thousands of victims who have suffered injustices and abuse of their basic rights and freedom and their voices are not being heard.

Positive change will not come from within the system because the "business men" who are controlling healthcare and social care are not interested in medicine and healing, they are too busy "reaching targets" and "making profits" and they are carrying out "the plan", which is created by powerful people in total secrecy. These people do not have the best interests of society as their main priority and they are receiving enormous salaries, while thousands of hospital patients, mental health patients, psychiatric patients, and care home residents are being mistreated and their human rights are being abused on a regular basis. Individuals need to take control of their medical treatment and the family members need to speak out on behalf of their loved ones to make sure that they receive proper care. We are living in a society, which is failing to look after UK citizens. Every day there are thousands of needless operations and harmful medical tests being carried out by local hospitals, as well as the use of ineffective vaccines, unsafe surgical procedures, and toxic drugs. There is too much reliance on invasive surgery and artificial chemical substances, which have a detrimental effect on the human body and there is a lack of compassion within the NHS.

The government and the local authorities will never be able to provide enough funding to meet the increasing demand because there are enormous debts and the public tax revenues are too low. Most of the money in circulation within the healthcare system and social care industry is being taken by private companies and private shareholders and this money is being invested into secret offshore bank accounts, which are outside the UK and owned by foreign hedge fund managers. Thousands of nurses, junior doctors, mental health workers, psychiatrists, GPs, and care workers have not been trained properly. The NHS is under extreme pressure and the social care sector is collapsing. The foundations of the system are not based upon medicine and wellbeing, they are based upon time, money, control, and procedure, as well as making huge profits that are not invested into improving the basic standard of healthcare and social care. The power of individuals within our society has been taken away and people are being told what to do by the large faceless private corporations who are trying to control every aspect of our lives and they are taking away our independence and freedom. The only thing that a person can ever truly own is their own body and nobody else has the right to decide when someone should die. Nature should be allowed to take its course and the doctors need to stop interfering with the human body. We have to rise up and take action. If we stay silent and do nothing the suffering will continue. We have to try to heal this broken system.

2

HUMAN RIGHTS ABUSE

Vulnerable individuals with complicated health conditions are having their freedom taken away by doctors and healthcare professionals. In reality the basic human rights of patients are being abused on a regular basis by the healthcare services, mental health services, and social care services. Old people with terminal diseases and old people with multiple health conditions are being abandoned. Young people with disabilities and learning difficulties and young people with mental health problems are being failed by the system. In many cases, doctors, nurses, healthcare workers, mental health clinicians, and care workers are ignoring the suffering of their patients and they are carrying out medical treatments, which are having a detrimental effect on the health of sick patients and the doctors are administering drugs and medicines, which have harmful side effects. Innocent young people are being detained inside the mental health wards and the psychiatric hospitals against their wishes and they are also being forced to accept prescriptions and injections of drugs, which are not safe for human consumption.

If a family member is terminally ill, every minute is precious and at this important time, they will need the support and care from doctors, nurses, and healthcare professionals, but in reality when a person is unwell, they are vulnerable and they can be manipulated by fear to accept medical treatment, which is not in their best interest and against their wishes. Intuition does not lie and sometimes we ignore it because we place our trust in consultant doctors and healthcare professionals. Unfortunately there are many UK doctors who are guilty of poor judgement. Psychiatrists and hospital doctors are making mistakes due to a lack of awareness and some doctors are prescribing medicines, which have been contaminated. When an individual is being given a toxic medicine, the family members have got two choices. They can stay silent and follow the advice of the doctor or they can speak out and stop the medical treatment and stop the prescription. In many cases, the unfortunate individual and the family members will decide to trust the doctor and this is a big mistake because the doctors are not being honest with the family members and they are carrying out the "NHS agenda", which is based upon "control and procedure". There is a lack of basic common sense and the agenda always comes first because this is the main priority within the small groups who are controlling the system.

In a situation where a consultant doctor is administering antibiotic medicine, which is poisoning the patient's body, that doctor will have to speak to the concerned family members who are aware of the serious situation. Unfortunately the doctors are not following the medical advice and in 99% of cases, they will choose to continue the prescription of the toxic medication. The doctors will refuse to accept that they have made an error because they do not want to admit that they have caused the death of a patient. When there is a premature death inside a hospital ward due to drug overdosage, the doctors will fail to record the real cause of the person's death because if the doctor accepts the evidence, it will prove that they ignored the medical warnings and harmful side effects caused by the medication. Elderly hospital outpatients are being given "orange coloured antibiotic tablets", while they are at home. All of the medicines are supposed to have been tested to make sure that they are safe, but in reality the side effects are extremely unpleasant and painful. The dangers of taking these drugs are much higher if you are over 75. When an elderly person is near to death due to the side effects of the drugs, the doctors will continue to administer the toxic antibiotics. The hospital doctors aren't available and there is a total lack of homecare because the government has cut social services by 80%. Old people are isolated and there is a complete lack of assistance and help because the district nurses are too busy. The district nurses are completely unaware of the fatal side effects because they don't recognise the signs of an allergic reaction caused by toxic antibiotic drugs. The GPs and district nurses are unaware of the symptoms and the doctors will continue to prescribe the "orange coloured antibiotic tablets" until the inevitable decline in health occurs and the person has passed away before their time. The hospital doctor will say that the person's death was "due to natural causes", but in reality the individual's right to life and liberty has been violated.

The national health service is controlled and run by Acute Trusts and there are 168 Acute Trusts, as well as over 200 clinical commissioning groups, which operate within the UK. There are 152 local council authorities and there are over 550 local hospitals in England. An independent report has found evidence of failings at every level within the NHS and there is widespread violation of human rights in hospitals, mental health units, psychiatric hospitals, nursing homes, dementia homes, and care homes. During 2017, more than 800 elderly hospital patients lost their lives due to dehydration and starvation due to a lack of care and every year hundreds of hospital patients and residents in care homes will die due to a lack of food and water. There are many more cases, which have not been investigated and the true numbers of preventable deaths have not been recorded accurately. There are thousands of individuals who are trapped inside overcrowded wards because there is a lack of social care provision and the delayed discharge of 30,000 able bodied UK pensioners has created total chaos inside the hospitals.

In the late 1990s, a medical professor together with his team, created a new care plan to improve the quality of care given to terminally ill patients and elderly patients who are close to death. The plan was named "The Liverpool Care Pathway" because it was developed by the Royal Liverpool University together with the Marie Curie Palliative Care Institute in Liverpool. The Liverpool Care Pathway (LCP) was created to help doctors and nurses to provide better quality end of life care and to raise the standard of palliative care, the new pathway was supposed to help people in the last few days and hours of their lifetime. The new care plan was adopted by the majority of NHS hospitals and within a few years, all of the hospitals were using the Liverpool Care Pathway. During the first five years of LCP there were some problems, but generally things were ok. Unfortunately the UK government decided to offer the hospitals financial incentives to use LCP and the managers decided to give staff members financial rewards in order to persuade them to use LCP to reach the new targets. The higher managers who were able to reach their targets, were given a large bonus and a large salary rise. Some of the higher managers created "death lists" and thousands of old people with minor health conditions and curable diseases, were put on the "death pathway" in order to reach the LCP targets and free up bed space in the overcrowded hospital wards. Doctors and nurses were forced by the managers to follow the new system and they were offered large financial rewards if they were able to achieve the LCP targets. In 2013, an independent report found evidence of widespread misuse of LCP in hospitals across the UK. The elderly population were "targeted" and sedated and denied food and fluids. Thousands of victims were sentenced to a premature death and more than 130,000 patients every year were put on the pathway and there is evidence of misuse of LCP in more than 60% of local hospitals.

Doctor John Ellershaw is a medical professor of palliative medicine and he led the team who created LCP. He issued a statement: "the Liverpool Care Pathway plan does not say that food and fluids should be withdrawn from a dying person, the doctors and the nurses are supposed to encourage sick patients to eat and drink small amounts of food and liquid and if they can't, they should be given liquid nutrition and fluid hydration". Unfortunately after the financial reward system was introduced some of the managers decided to create the "death pathway" and the elderly who had many months left to live were put on the "pathway". The elderly who were trying to recover were also put on the "pathway". Old people with curable diseases and minor infections were put on the "pathway" against their wishes and a large number of hospital managers, doctors, and nurses were guilty of carrying out mass euthanasia. The junior doctors were forced to decide if a person should be put on the "death list" or not and they were left without any help from the consultant doctors who were busy working in the A & E departments.

The "death pathway" is a very simple two step process. Step 1: heavy sedation using large doses of diamorphine. Step 2: removal of food and fluid tubes and the withdrawal of life saving drugs. LCP is supposed to be used in the last days and hours of a person's life, but in reality there were thousands of UK citizens who were put on the "death pathway" for the last 2 to 3 weeks of their lifetime. Hospital patients should be allowed to pass away with dignity and in thousands of cases, people were subjected to starvation and dehydration. The elderly were given powerful sedatives and could not communicate with their family members and relatives. Thousands of individuals were not told about the decision to put them on the "pathway" and in more than 50% of the cases, the medical staff did not tell the family members that the decision had been taken to put their loved ones on the "pathway". There is absolutely no excuse or justification for this kind of cruelty and there are hundreds of managers, doctors, and nurses who are guilty of manslaughter and they are still working in healthcare in the UK and abroad. The NHS is guilty of crimes against humanity and thousands of elderly victims have not come forward because they are scared of the system.

A decision was made in 2014, to ban the use of the Liverpool Care Pathway due to widespread misuse of LCP and there is evidence to prove that the local hospitals and the doctors were still using the banned practice of LCP during 2015, under a different name. In 2017, new guidelines for "hospital end of life care" were introduced and the new guidelines are exactly the same as the LCP "death pathway" system. The staff nurses have been given permission to use powerful sedatives without having to call for a doctor to get permission and validation. The medical staff have been advised to identify certain signs and changes and if an individual shows any signs of "fatigue" and "agitation", they can be put on the "withdrawal pathway", which involves the removal of the food tubes and the fluid tubes followed by heavy sedation where the person will not wake up again. In some situations where the person is lifeless, this is the most humane action, but in a situation where someone has a 90% chance of making a full recovery, it is a crime against the individual. You cannot diagnose dying because many sick patients will recover from a disease or an illness. "Fatigue" and "agitation" are not reliable indicators and they should not be used in diagnosis. The NHS is guilty of mistreating the elderly. Hospitals are causing unnecessary pain and suffering by needlessly prolonging life, instead of allowing the patient to pass away with dignity. People are being subjected to invasive and painful medical testing and medical treatment, which hastens death. In reality vulnerable individuals are being put on the "withdrawal pathway" and sentenced to a premature death in order to fulfil "the plan" and hospital managers and healthcare professionals are failing the elderly population.

In 2013, a 90 year old woman went into a local hospital in southeast England for treatment of a minor injury and after a few days inside the ward she developed pneumonia. The doctors made a decision to put the patient on the Liverpool Care Pathway and food and fluids were withdrawn, the family members were not told about the decision to put their loved one on the "pathway". The doctors and nurses told the upset family members that the patient has 48 hours left to live and the woman was not told that she had been put on the "pathway". The family were suspicious and they knew that something was wrong. When they visited the hospital, they found that their loved one had been sedated. When she woke up, the woman asked for food and water and she was refused by the medical staff who tried to tell the concerned family members that the patient's physical body was "shutting down" due to her age and they had decided to put her on the Liverpool Pathway. The family confronted the doctors and the healthcare professionals. The confused patient was taken off the "pathway" immediately and she was allowed food and water. After a short time the woman recovered and she was discharged from hospital and she is now enjoying the rest of her life with family and friends. This may sound unbelievable, but unfortunately it is 100% true.

An 85 year old woman went into a local hospital in Cambridge for treatment in 2011. The woman had been suffering from the effects of a heart attack and although she was very ill, she was not ready to pass away. The woman was holding on because she wanted to spend some more time with her family and relatives before passing away. The doctor said that the patient would not survive for more than three days without food and water and they were putting the patient on the Liverpool Pathway against the wishes of the family. The woman was not ready to die and she survived for twelve days without food or water and before passing away, she was left in a state of distress and confusion. During the last twelve days of her life, this unfortunate individual received no food or fluid or medication and this kind of illegal medical procedure should be banned. Starvation and dehydration are supposed to be against the law, but unfortunately this has become common practice inside hospitals and care homes. In reality the elderly are being denied food and water, while they are dying and this is completely unacceptable. There are many thousands of UK pensioners who are having their human rights and freedom taken away by the system on a regular basis and the family members need to stand up and speak out to protect their loved ones.

We are not living in a democracy. Democracy is an illusion used by the politicians and the people in power. The doctors are using coercion and control and the elderly are being kept inside hospital wards against their wishes. Young people who have mental health problems and learning disabilities are being locked up inside mental health wards and psychiatric wards because they have been abandoned by the system. The elderly are dying in front of the other visitors and patients in the hospital wards because they are not allowed to go home and pass away with their family and this is happening on a daily basis. If a person has six months or more left of their lifetime and they are given an antibiotic drug and within three weeks that person dies suddenly due to liver failure and heart failure caused by toxic drugs, you would have to say that there is something seriously wrong with the national health service. The giant pharmaceutical companies are releasing life threatening chemical substances into the local pharmacy networks and millions of people are being given poor quality medicines. There are many thousands of cases, where the NHS has damaged the health of an individual by administering harmful drugs.

The elderly population are trapped inside a dysfunctional system, which is failing a large number of UK citizens. There are a lot of problems, which need sorting out and we hear about it every day in the news. The NHS is neglecting people, the system is taking away our freedom, and people are being given toxic medication. The doctors and nurses are unaware of the side effects and they are responsible for causing a lot of needless suffering. There is a total lack of compassion within the healthcare system and social care industry and many people have been abandoned. When you can't take care of yourself, you are at the mercy of the system and this system has no mercy. The workers are busy following guidelines created by the higher managers and the needs of young people and old people are being ignored. Mental health patients and psychiatric patients who are disturbed are being imprisoned and they are carrying out self harm and this is not acceptable. The situation has reached the point where many NHS professionals are unable to comprehend the permanent damage and lifelong injury caused by bad healthcare, which has been administered by people who refuse to accept the "painful reality" of their irresponsible careless actions. The family members of individuals who have been subjected to "medical abuse" causing the loss of life have got to live with the pain and grief forever and they are supposed to carry on as if nothing has happened. This is shameful and disgraceful and it has to be stopped. When a person is in a desperate situation there are some people who will use this as a justification for inflicting cruelty upon the helpless. This is unforgivable and there are a lot of doctors who are unable to accept reality when someone is dying and they will administer stronger drugs in a false attempt to prolong the life of the unfortunate individual. In most cases, the drugs don't work and they cause damage and injury inside the major organs in the physical body. If a doctor has made a mistake, this will cause unnecessary suffering. When a doctor is guilty of a serious error of judgement, it is time for the family members to take control of the situation because doctors, nurses, clinicians, psychiatrists, GPs, and social care workers are carrying out human rights abuse.

3

PATIENTS ARE BEING TERMINATED

This is a very disturbing statement, which sounds like a "conspiracy theory", but unfortunately I have all the necessary evidence to prove that this is happening on a regular basis inside hospitals, psychiatric hospitals, mental health hospitals, care homes, and nursing homes. There is a nationwide problem with specialist dementia care homes because there are a lot of homes where the specialists have not been given any training and residents and family members are being told lies. The managers and the supervisors are breaking the law because hundreds of staff members have not received any training and the residents are being neglected, while they are deteriorating and there are large numbers of preventable deaths happening on a regular basis inside specialist dementia care homes.

There is a group of individuals who are experiencing violent hypersensitive/allergic reactions caused by antibiotic drugs. These individuals cannot tolerate the acids and chemicals, which are contained within the tablets. Some antibiotic drugs have been contaminated and they are extremely poisonous due to the nature of the chemical agents in the medicine. These drugs are toxic and they are not allowed to be given to children and this is because they are unsafe. Hypersensitivity is passed on to children by the parents DNA and there are some lucky people who are able to tolerate drugs, which cause allergic reactions. In reality UK hospital patients with respiratory diseases are being neglected, while they are suffering and they are being given unsafe medicines. The hospital doctors are unaware of the side effects and the pharmaceutical industry is a money making machine because their main priority is "making profit". The healthcare needs of vulnerable individuals are being ignored and sick patients are being given substances, which the physical body cannot digest properly and the drugs also cause chronic acid indigestion.

Antibiotic medicines are supposed to fight bacterial infections by destroying the infected cells, which are in the patient's body, but in reality these powerful medicines also destroy the healthy cells inside the liver and kidneys. Antibiotic drugs need to use the bloodstream to transport the medicine to the place where all the diseased cells are located. Unfortunately there is a problem here. Some antibiotic drugs can cause damage to the major organs and they also destroy the natural enzymes in the liver and the healthy bacteria in the stomach. When an outpatient is experiencing an allergic reaction caused by prescription medicine, the medical advice is very clear: "stop taking the medicine immediately and see a doctor or a healthcare professional", but in reality the consultant doctors are not following this advice and guidance and harmful prescription drugs are being given to outpatients by the local GP surgeries and old people are suffering, while they are at home. Large numbers of elderly outpatients are being admitted into hospitals with problems caused by the side effects and some of the effects can be fatal because the drugs can cause rapid deterioration of the liver and acute liver failure. When a person is in this condition, they will not survive for very long and the outcome is inevitable. This is a crime against the elderly and it is happening on a daily basis inside hospitals, mental health units, psychiatric wards, care homes, nursing homes, and specialist dementia homes. When you have reached the age of 65, the doctors will try to take control of your health and your care, but in reality there is too much control and there is a complete lack of care. The truth is being hidden and if an elderly patient has more than six months left of their lifetime, the NHS will always choose the "cheap option" and in many cases, the unfortunate individual will be sentenced to an unnecessary and premature death caused by toxic prescription drugs and a lack of care.

Independent scientific research has discovered the truth about the toxicity and contamination of the chemicals, which are inside prescription medicines. Some of the medicines contain chemical agents and corrosive acids, which destroy the soft tissues inside the physical body and cause damage to the healthy cells in the stomach.

Toxic substances have a detrimental effect on the vital functions of the human immune system. The drug companies are creating harmful medicines and they are making huge amounts of money and there is evidence of corruption inside many pharmaceutical drug companies. There are more than one million victims in different countries around the world who have died prematurely, there are large numbers of deaths caused by toxic medicines and it is not possible to calculate the true number of fatalities accurately. You cannot trust the scientists inside the laboratories who work for the big pharmaceutical giants because they do not care about humanity, they have destroyed the blueprint of mother nature in order to make a profit and they are breaking the law. People are being given drugs, which are not suitable for human use and this is illegal. Doctors in the USA and doctors in Germany have started speaking out against the global drug industry and the families of UK victims are also beginning to speak out against the national health service. The NHS is stuck in the past and it is outdated and there are many other european countries where people are receiving better quality healthcare and safe social care.

Prescription medicines come with a warning leaflet inside the box and there are a lot of details and medical advice, as well as the warnings about the dangers of side effects. There are hundreds of harmful side effects caused by prescription drugs and there is widespread corruption within the commercial drug industry. Some of the companies are producing ineffective drugs, which are being released into the global healthcare market. There is a massive problem within global healthcare and millions of patients are consuming toxic drugs. Hepatotoxicity is a medical term for "chemical driven liver damage" and drug induced liver failure causes thousands of premature deaths every year all around the world. There are a lot of medical drugs that can cause hepatic liver failure and hepatitis. More than 75% of unexpected patient deaths are due to acute liver failure caused by hepatic injury due to harmful chemicals. Man made chemical agents are being administered by doctors and nurses and these drugs are harmful because they contain noxious substances, which cause injury and illness. The pharmaceutical drug industry is poisoning millions of people and the politicians and the government are failing to protect UK citizens. There is a lack of awareness and understanding within mainstream medicine and mainstream science regarding toxins and toxicity. NHS doctors and British scientists are unaware of hepatotoxicity, which is caused by contaminated prescription drugs and they are guilty of a lack of intelligence.

Here is a list of prescription medicines, which cause hepatotoxicity: antibiotic drugs, anti-inflammatory drugs, anti-depressant drugs, anti-leptic drugs for epilepsy, anti-psychotic drugs, asthma and bronchitis drugs, drugs for multiple sclerosis, drugs for attention deficit disorder, and drugs for thought disorders. The majority of private drug companies are producing noxious substances. Doctors, psychiatrists, clinicians, and GPs are giving people harmful chemicals and they don't recognise the detrimental effects. There are three main types of chronic liver failure caused by hepatotoxicity. 1. Failure due to medical drug allergy and hypersensitive reaction. 2. Failure due to medical drug overdosage. 3. Failure due to hepatitis and severe hepatic injury. The physical body cannot absorb the chemicals in the drugs because of their toxic nature and the side effects cause damage to the human central nervous system. The drugs contain corrosive acids and chemical agents, which destroy the vital membranes and essential proteins inside the physical body. The drugs also destroy vital enzymes in the liver, as well as the mitochondria and they cause damage to the immune system. After the drugs have entered the bloodstream they become "extremely reactive" as they turn into "toxic metabolites" and in many cases, the chemicals in the drugs will be excreted in the bile because the physical body cannot digest the drugs. Toxic drugs are not fat soluble and they don't mix well with other medicines and they are being prescribed for young people with mental health problems and old people with multiple conditions, against the wishes of the unfortunate individuals.

Hepatocellular injury is a medical term for "serious and chronic damage to cells in the body caused by drugs". When an individual is taking a medicine, which is causing hepatic damage, as well as other medications, they will not survive. The drugs mix together, creating "a deadly cocktail" of chemicals that cause acute liver failure and death. There is an antibiotic medicine, which is being prescribed by hospital doctors and its name is Isoniazid and it should be withdrawn from circulation within the global healthcare system. Thousands of individuals have experienced severe side effects and the NHS is using INH Therapy (isoniazid treatment) in the local hospitals to treat individuals with bacterial infections. INH Therapy is being administered by doctors in different countries around the world and there is independent medical evidence of brain damage and the destruction of nerve cells caused by isoniazid and it can also cause blindness, nerve damage, seizures, cell destruction, renal failure, liver failure, heart failure, and death.

Hospital staff have been given basic lifesaving training and consultant surgeons have carried out lifesaving operations. Consultant doctors have carried out lifesaving medical procedures and this is the light side of the NHS. Unfortunately there is also a dark side and UK citizens are dying before their time because there is a lack of care and attention. The NHS is guilty of: misdiagnosis, failing to recognise harmful side effects caused by drugs, failing to carry out medical tests, failing to act upon test results, administering toxic drugs, administering too many unnecessary drugs, and prescribing drugs, which cause allergic chemical reactions. The doctors and nurses are allowing the health of the elderly to deteriorate and they are carrying out pointless medical procedures. Mistakes and errors can lead to the premature death of a patient and this is happening on a regular basis inside local hospitals across the country. In the last five years thousands of residential care homes and nursing homes have closed and this has put unbearable pressure on doctors and nurses due to the overcrowded wards. Some doctors have decided to use the "withdrawal pathway" in order to hasten the death of vulnerable individuals. In reality the doctors are breaking the law and they are denying the truth.

In 2014, an elderly woman went into a local hospital in Hampshire for treatment of a kidney infection. After a few days she was recovering in an elderly ward after a successful treatment of the condition and the doctor decided to put her on the "death pathway". The unfortunate individual was given a large dose of diamorphine by a syringe driver, which automatically pumps the sedative into the patient's bloodstream and the food tubes and fluid tubes were removed. 48 hours later, the woman died due to a lack of food and water and her family were devastated. The family were suspicious and they decided to take action and they started a public campaign to raise awareness about the cruelty and abuse, which is happening inside many UK hospitals. The hospital claimed that the woman's death was due to her existing medical condition and they tried to hide the truth. In reality the family members know what really happened to their loved one and thanks to their campaign the truth has come out. There are local hospitals where people are being sentenced to an unnecessary death because they have been put on the "pathway" and this kind of cruel treatment is widespread within the healthcare service.

The global pharmaceutical giants are carrying out illegal clinical trials in order to get their products into the market place because they know that some of their drugs are unsafe. The drug companies are trying to use secret clinical trials to bypass the law and they are releasing large numbers of toxic drugs into the local pharmacies around the UK. The NHS has become like a machine and it has got a lot of advanced technology and scientific knowledge, which is not being used properly. The system is far too dogmatic and there is a total lack of flexibility and adaptability. Doctors and nurses are not allowed to use their intuition because the managers and chief executives have created a hostile working environment and the hospital staff are not looking after the patients because there is a serious lack of available time. There are many situations where the family members have to sit and watch their loved one who is suffering because they are being neglected and they are not receiving proper care and attention. Previous governments and local authorities have invested billions of pounds into the economy and most of this money has not reached the areas where it is needed most because the cash has been invested into numerous invisible offshore bank accounts controlled by large corporations and private companies who run the NHS providers and the social care providers. If you are elderly, you cannot trust in the system because old people are being forgotten. Thousands of victims have died and there is a nationwide failure of the duty of care.

When a person is dying in a hospital ward, most doctors will continue to administer toxic drugs in order to hasten the death and this is not acceptable. Critically ill elderly hospital patients must be allowed to return to their homes if it is possible, so that they can spend some precious time with their loved ones. The doctors and healthcare professionals are not providing any "end of life" care and there are more than 250,000 UK pensioners who have had their lifespan shortened by the negligent actions of NHS consultants. There is a lack of respect for old people within the national health service, mental health service, and the social care service. There are thousands of family members who are having to fight against the system to stop decisions being made by the doctors, which are not in the person's best interest. If the family decide to stay silent the doctors will continue to carry out harmful medical treatment and large numbers of the elderly population will be sentenced to an unnecessary death. Just because someone is old, it does not mean that their right to life should be disregarded and violated by staff and healthcare professionals. Hospital doctors and medical staff are using fear tactics against the family members who are trying to stop the mistreatment of their loved ones, so that they can take them home where they are safe from harm. The family members who have placed their trust in the NHS have been told lies and their loved ones have been sent to a painful death by doctors and nurses who are guilty of medical negligence.

Consultant doctors and junior doctors are guilty of poor judgement and a lack of awareness and they are responsible for sending thousands of elderly pensioners to a premature death every year. There are many complex health problems, which old people suffer from and there is a lack of care and compassion within hospitals and care homes. The national health service is in crisis and the social care sector is collapsing. Large numbers of medical staff and care workers have not been trained and there is a staffing crisis within every area of healthcare, mental healthcare, and social care. It shouldn't matter if you are young, middle aged, or elderly. People have the right to receive treatment, which has health benefits and the possibility of life extension, but unfortunately there are many thousands of UK citizens who are having treatments, which shorten the lifespan of the unfortunate person. When an elderly person's death has been caused by prescription drug poisoning, the cause of death will be recorded as "death due to natural causes". The real cause of death will not be mentioned in the person's official medical documents, which are signed by the consultant doctors. There is large scale abuse of patients being carried out on a daily basis and the managers are allowing this to happen inside local hospitals, mental health hospitals, psychiatric hospitals, specialist dementia units, disability units, care homes, and nursing homes.

There are many different ways to send a frail elderly person to a premature death and elderly patients are being mistreated and ignored every day inside hospitals around the UK. GP doctors and district nurses are administering chemical agents and people are being given noxious substances, instead of medicine. We are living in an unfair world where we are being told lies and it is time to stop calling these substances "medicine" because they are not medicinal or beneficial in any way, shape, or form. We are being used like guinea pigs and mice in a "laboratory experiment" carried out by corrupt companies and suspicious scientists. The consultants and the clinicians cannot be trusted anymore, so it is up to the individual to take responsibility and control of their treatment. We have reached a sorry state of affairs where human lives are being disregarded and cut short because the medical staff are being put under extreme pressure. When a person passes away in suspicious circumstances it leaves a dark stain within the soul of the family members. If a doctor has made an error and they are unaware of their mistake, this is unavoidable. When a doctor has made an error and they are aware of their mistake and they continue to follow NHS procedure, this is abuse. Good intentions can be harmful when a healthcare professional has made a serious error of judgement. In reality there is far too much cruelty within the national health service and vulnerable patients are being terminated.

4

CORRUPT MANAGEMENT

Making money is the main priority. The people who control the NHS and the private social care sector and the directors who run the drug companies are making millions of pounds, while thousands of individuals are suffering because they are not being looked after properly. The people who are in power have got a lot of questions to answer and they are responsible for most of the problems in the healthcare service and social care sector. Hospitals are full of sick patients and the healthcare system has become like a disease industry. Money is the controlling influence and the managers and the chief executives are the ones at the top of the money tree. Some chief executives have been given a £35,000 annual pay rise and this is more than double a nurses average salary. The average salary for a nurse is £16,000 a year and top nurses can earn up to £28,000 a year. The average salary for a chief is £160,000 and top chiefs can earn up to £280,000 a year. The maths are simple. Add a zero to your salary and you are rich. The greedy business barons who control the big private social care providers are making millions of pounds in profits and there are many thousands of care home residents who are being neglected every day and they are not receiving any care. Independent reports and police investigations have found evidence of the abuse of patients within the NHS and the social care industry.

The national health service is losing huge sums of money every year and millions of pounds have been wasted by the hospital managers. In February 2018, the NHS trusts were more than £1.2 billion in debt and in May 2018, NHS trusts recorded a deficit of £960 million. There is one trust, which recorded debts of £40 million and the economists say that the debt level and the deficit level will rise in the near future. The managers and chief executives have been rewarded, while the trusts have lost millions of pounds because there is widespread incompetence at the top within healthcare management. The owners of the big private companies who provide social care have made millions in profits, while the social care industry has massive debts and the local authorities cannot afford to fund social care properly because they have run out of money. We are living in a corrupt society where nurses and care workers have been forced to accept the 1% pay cap, while managers, chief executives, and the owners of the private care providers have received enormous pay rises every year. The healthcare industry and the social care industry are obsessed with advertising and marketing. The "happy images", which are everywhere inside hospitals and care homes are an illusion. In reality there is a total lack of resources inside hospitals, mental health hospitals, psychiatric hospitals, specialist care homes, nursing homes, and private residential care homes. The staff members have not been trained properly and some of the medical staff have not received any training at all. The elderly are being abused every day and there are thousands of preventable deaths due to negligence every year. Elderly patients, mental health patients, and care home residents are not being supervised properly and they are being abandoned by the system.

Thousands of old people are trapped inside overcrowded hospital wards because there is a lack of social care and there are too many old people in care homes and nursing homes because the family members cannot look after their elderly parents and relatives. Most of the nurses and the care workers are trying to do their best to look after hospital patients and care home residents, but in reality they can't provide any care because they are under too much pressure. Hospital nurses and care workers are not treated with respect by the managers and they are not allowed to speak out if they are unhappy with poor working conditions and low wages. Nurses and care workers are being bullied and there is a culture of intimidation and hostility within healthcare management and social care management. Some managers behave like angry dictators and they will try to intimidate and bully their staff members. Any staff member who speaks out will be fired or suspended immediately. There are many managers who have had to retire early because of mental health problems due to obsessive compulsive disorder, anxiety neurosis, and depression. The managers spend too much time thinking about healthcare protocols and hitting their targets and they are disconnected from reality. The healthcare system is broken and the social care system is collapsing due to an increasing lack of funding and the funding crisis has been created by government spending cuts and millions of pounds are being wasted every year. The social care sector and the NHS trusts are being "dominated" by big private business corporations and the agenda has been created by the managers and the politicians. Hospital managers are creating healthcare systems, which are based around "cost and time" and they have sacrificed "quality care" because "money and greed" are the main drivers within the healthcare industry.

In 2015, an independent report carried out by NHS England revealed some shocking and disturbing details. Southern Health NHS Foundation Trust was found guilty by the coroners of neglecting people and failing in its duty of care, the trust was also found guilty of failing to investigate the unexpected deaths of hundreds of patients with learning disabilities and mental health problems. Southern Health is one of the largest mental health providers in the country and it has hospitals in most of the counties in the south of the UK. The coroners said that the trust had neglected people and failed to investigate their deaths. Young people with learning disabilities and old people with mental health problems were ignored and their human rights were abused. During 2011 to 2015, there were more than 1,500 unexpected deaths and most of them were preventable. The management team at Southern Health failed to investigate the deaths because the managers knew that vulnerable individuals had been abandoned by the staff. Only 1% of unexpected deaths of disabled young people with learning disabilities were investigated and only 0.3% of unexpected deaths of old people with mental health problems were investigated. There is evidence and proof of staff mistreating patients and the managers are trying to hide the truth. Southern Health are guilty of medical negligence and there is a total lack of leadership and authority.

Across the country there are mental health trusts and mental health providers who are failing thousands of UK citizens every year because there is a shortage of local services. Traumatised individuals are finding it impossible to get help and some people are committing suicide because they have lost hope and they are depressed. There is a nationwide shortage of inpatient units, mental health wards, acute wards, mental health hospitals, GP services, and ambulance services. The NHS is in desperate need of 6,000 more mental health nurses and many nurses have not been given the correct training in how to deal with psychiatric patients with mental health conditions and disabilities. In 2017, the coroners issued 136 "warnings" that were sent to the private mental health providers because they were failing far too many people. The psychiatrists and the mental health clinicians are prescribing large doses of anti-psychotics and anti-depressants and they do not care about the harmful side effects because they have decided to trust the scientists who work for the drug industry, which is responsible for producing noxious chemicals. People with mental illness and people with disabilities are being failed by healthcare professionals who are supposed to provide good quality care.

More than 15 million UK citizens will experience a mental health problem every year and the crisis is getting worse every day. In 2017, there were record levels of violence and abuse against patients in mental health wards and psychiatric wards and more than 5,000 incidents were investigated including hundreds of suicides, dozens of murders, and thousands of cases of self harm. The mental health system is failing young people, middle aged people, and old people. The system is not fit for purpose and there were more than 17,000 cases of disturbed individuals assaulting and attacking the other inmates inside mental health wards and mental health hospitals during 2017. The system is under extreme pressure and the workforce is overstretched because there is a UK shortage of doctors, mental health staff, and psychiatric nurses. The staff members have not been given enough training and they don't understand mental health issues. People who have psychosis, schizophrenia, anxiety, depression, thought disorders, personality disorders, autism, and asperger's syndrome are being subjected to discrimination. They are being mistreated and given an incorrect medical diagnosis and drugs, which have been contaminated. People with mental health conditions who are in desperate need of help are being traumatised by mental health staff and people with psychiatric conditions who are violent and disturbed are being abused by psychiatric staff. A recent independent report has revealed a worrying rise in attacks against mental health staff and psychiatric staff carried out by NHS patients and thousands of staff members are suffering every day. There were around 42,000 reported cases of mental health workers being attacked during 2017. Medical staff are busy picking up the pieces of a broken system and every day there are many situations where they are failing to look after people. In reality large numbers of staff members are guilty of medical negligence.

The local authorities have found evidence of large scale corruption within the private mental health providers and there is absence of intelligence within mental health trust management. There is a big problem within our society regarding domestic abuse and institutional abuse and the NHS is also guilty of carrying out human rights abuse. There is evidence of endemic abuse and violation of the Mental Health Act (MHA). The Mental Health Act is being used by psychiatric staff to deny people their freedom and innocent individuals are being imprisoned inside psychiatric wards by staff when they pose no threat to society and the community. Mental health patients and psychiatric patients are being forcibly injected with addictive anti-psychotic drugs, which increase anxiety and confusion within the individual and people are being forced to accept harmful medical treatment. There is a restraining method being used by staff in mental health hospitals and psychiatric hospitals and it is called prone restraint. Prone restraint involves forcing a person face down onto the ground, while force and pressure are applied by two or more staff members. This restraining method can cause injury and death and it is physical abuse. Young people with mental health problems who are in hospital for treatment are not receiving any care and they are being treated like prisoners and they are being deprived of their liberty. During 2016, more than 600 incidents happened within six months where prone restraint was used to control vulnerable young people inside St Andrew's Mental Health Hospital in Northampton.

St Andrew's Mental Healthcare is supposed to be a "specialist mental health provider" and it has been involved in a scandal involving young people who need help. St Andrew's provides mental healthcare for NHS patients and it has four large hospitals in the UK and it is charging the NHS £220,000 a year for each patient including a £3,000 top up fee. Health regulators and the government have criticised the hospital in Northampton and the media are investigating the hospital and the provider. The police have found evidence of disturbing conditions inside the hospital. Independent investigations into complaints made by the parents of the victims have uncovered evidence of systemic abuse. Young people with learning difficulties were subjected to a "behaviour management system", which is cruel and unfair and they were locked inside their rooms for long periods of time and their freedom was taken away. Some individuals were not allowed outside and they were banned from entering into public areas within the hospital and they did not understand what was expected of them. Youngsters who failed to follow the house rules were excluded and subjected to isolation for long periods of time for more than several weeks. The distressed individuals were given large doses of toxic psychiatric drugs and they were not allowed to see their parents. Some young people became clinically obese and they were kept inside and not allowed to exercise because they did not follow the house rules. The hospital staff members were using "tough discipline" in an attempt to treat teenagers who have learning difficulties and behavioural problems and they are failing hundreds of young people. Teenagers with mental health problems were being abused and neglected on a regular basis inside the hospital and the truth is still coming out. In 2016, the hospital earned more than £200 million in profits and the top chief executive received a salary of £590,000. Vulnerable young individuals have been abandoned and failed by mental health staff who have not been trained and there is a total lack of organisation and leadership within the managers and executives who run St Andrew's Mental Healthcare.

Thousands of incidents of abuse against patients in psychiatric hospitals and mental health hospitals have been investigated in different areas around the UK including Scotland, Wales, Devon, Yorkshire, Hampshire, Surrey, Sussex, Dorset, Cornwall, and the Midlands. In 2017, the amount of reported cases carried out by NHS staff has doubled and during 2016, there were more than 500 incidents inside local hospitals. In reality there are thousands of cases, which have not been reported or investigated because the victims are too afraid to report the perpetrators. A survey carried out by independent health regulators has found evidence of routine neglect and abuse within the mental health system and 75% of mental health workers say that people are not being looked after properly by the staff. More than 80% of the staff said that they could not provide any care or therapy because they did not have enough time. Patients with mental health conditions are having to wait for too long and they are not receiving any treatment or help, while they are waiting. Patients with psychiatric conditions are being forced to accept medical treatment against their wishes and the doctors and nurses are administering too many drugs. In many cases, the drugs being used are unsafe and people are being forcibly drugged and sedated by doctors and mental health professionals. Thousands of disturbed individuals are being subjected to psychiatric abuse in psychiatric wards and there is evidence of misdiagnosis, forced drugging, unnecessary medical procedures, unlawful detention, and the use of violence and physical abuse to control the patients. The mental healthcare system is full of needless suffering and you have to ask the question: why is this happening in a rich country? It is happening because there is widespread corruption within healthcare management, social care management, private care providers, and mental health trusts and this is deeply disturbing.

The top managers within the NHS and the owners of the big private social care providers are obsessed with making money. Hospital car parks and hospital shops are more than double the price of a normal car park and a normal shop. Many care home residents and nursing home residents are paying the providers £1,000 a week and they are living in homes where they are not safe. Old people are being left alone for long periods of time, while they are suffering and in pain. The local authorities have invested billions of pounds into healthcare and social care and more than 90% of this money has been taken by the private companies, pharmaceutical corporations, and the private social care providers. The chancellor and the government will have to print a lot of new money and this new money must be free of interest payments and debts because the global banking system is full of corruption and greed. People are living like prisoners trapped inside the false economy of cash creation and money supply and the

UK economy is being dominated by a cycle of borrowing and debt. The hedge fund managers and the multinational pharmaceutical corporations have got complete control of the marketplace and the market is you and me.

The drug companies are making billions in profits and millions of people are being given ineffective drugs that don't work. The doctors need to realize that they still have a lot to learn about drug allergies and hypersensitivity and there is a total lack of care inside hospitals, mental health hospitals, psychiatric hospitals, residential care homes, nursing homes, and specialist dementia care homes. The managers who are running the healthcare industry and the owners of the big private care providers are being paid huge salaries, while nurses and care workers are receiving the minimum wage. The people who crave power and wealth are the same ones who are unable to use it wisely and the people at the top are failing to provide vital services, which are supposed to save the lives of critically ill individuals. Higher managers, company directors, and corporate executives have become greedy and arrogant and the staff members are not treated with respect. Liberty, honesty, and intelligence are the foundations of good health and good care. We need to rise up and stop this corrupt management.

5

SUPPRESSING THE TRUTH

Healthcare managers and social care managers are covering up failure inside hospitals and residential care homes and the truth is being hidden. The system is failing thousands of patients and residents and there is a lack of care and compassion. People are being ignored when they are in pain due to the lack of staff and some people are being abused and mistreated by angry staff members and hostile care nurses. Many junior doctors, mental health staff, and GPs have not been trained properly and there are nurses working in the care industry and they are neglecting the residents. More than 50% of the staff who work in the care industry have not been trained and they are not aware of the care plan. The care plan was designed to give people better quality healthcare with health benefits and life extension, but in reality there are thousands of hospital staff and care workers who are not following the care plan. The national health service and the social care industry are being controlled by large business corporations and there is a lack of regulation and accountability. Private companies and greedy people have made billions of pounds in profits and the money has not been invested into improving the standard of healthcare and medical treatment. When a patient's death has been caused by suspicious circumstances, the local NHS trust will carry out a hospital investigation into the circumstances of the unexpected death. Unfortunately in the majority of cases, the truth will remain hidden and the family members will be left in the dark. When you are traumatised and consumed by grief, the truth is the only light that you can see in the darkness. The truth can't heal the pain inside, but it helps the human mind to come to terms with the death of a loved one.

The family and relatives who can't understand what has happened to their loved one are left in a state of anger and confusion and there is evidence of a widespread cover up taking place within the healthcare service.

Truth is like medicine. It might be unpleasant, but it must be swallowed. When the unnecessary death of a patient has been caused by prescription drugs and a lack of care, this will not be recorded in the medical documents and official paperwork. When all of the papers have been completed and signed by the doctor, important details are left out and they are not recorded on any of the documents. In reality there is dishonesty within the NHS and the social care industry. The managers and chief executives will take action to stop the truth from coming out because they will lose their jobs and their reputations will be damaged. The managers and owners of the private social care providers do not want the truth to come out because they will be forced to carry out an internal investigation by the local authority and the police. Powerful people are being protected from prosecution and they are breaking the law. The medical records of deceased individuals are being altered and falsified in order to hide the evidence of medical negligence. The truth is being erased from the national medical records every day inside hospitals and care homes. The "perfect images" portrayed inside hospitals and care homes are not based upon reality. If you look at the outside of a hospital building you will see large areas where all of the rooms have been abandoned and the outside walls are covered with dirt and grime. We are the consumers in a commercial industry and there are many thousands of hospital patients and care home residents who are being forced to sit in a chair all day and this is very bad for the blood circulation and the heart. Doctors and nurses have got access to advanced technology and scientific knowledge, which can be used to diagnose and treat people, but in reality the junior doctors and the junior nurses don't know how to operate important lifesaving equipment and there is a lack of common sense and basic intelligence inside hospitals and care homes.

There are around 21,500 residential care homes, nursing homes, and specialist homes across the country. The social care industry is worth £17.5 billion and there are 1.5 million UK citizens who require home care and there are roughly 450,000 UK pensioners who live in residential care homes around the country. The social care sector is not fit for purpose and the system is failing thousands of elderly patients, disabled patients, and patients with mental health problems. Large numbers of care home residents and nursing home residents are paying more than £1,000 a week and they are receiving poor quality care and harmful medical treatment. In 2017, there were 6,000 reported incidents of neglect and abuse of old people in the social care sector. Every day there are more incidents happening and there are individuals who are being neglected inside care homes, nursing homes, and specialist homes for old people with disabilities and dementia. Thousands of residents are too afraid to complain and they are not able to report the perpetrators. Many incidents of neglect and abuse have not been investigated and some of the private care home managers are failing to investigate thousands of cases of preventable death every year. The truth is shocking. More than 60% of care homes and nursing homes are unsafe and more than 100,000 UK citizens are living in hazardous surroundings because the managers are not providing proper safeguarding.

The social care industry is being dominated by a small number of large private companies and the social care sector has got a deficit of £1.5 billion. HC-ONE has 350 homes and debts of £500 million, Four Seasons has 340 homes and debts of £450 million, Care UK has 114 homes and debts of £80 million. There are 5,500 care home providers and most of them are small in size. The care industry is in crisis and the system is collapsing due to greed and a lack of leadership, the large providers who own hundreds of homes and the small private providers who own 1 or 2 homes are not looking after their "customers" properly, the basic standard of care is unacceptable and there is a lack of resources and funding. Some of the care workers and nurses have not been given any training and they are not following the Mental Capacity Act (MCA), which is supposed to protect mental health patients from human rights abuse. Social care workers and nurses cannot afford the cost of living and this is the reality within our modern society. Private companies are using the private equity system in order to transfer billions of pounds into foreign offshore companies and secret bank accounts, which are controlled by foreign owners and hedge fund managers. The directors of private companies who own the big social care providers are stealing huge sums of public money. The managers are being paid far too much money and they are using financial accountants who are creating elaborate tax avoidance schemes and the company directors are receiving massive pay rises every year. The majority of residential care homes are being run by foreign owners and commercial business barons who have no understanding of social care because their main priority is making large profits. Every year the big private providers are making huge profits and at the end of the year the profits become massive debts after all the bills have been paid, while the company directors are receiving enormous salaries and an annual bonus of more than £50,000, as well as other financial rewards. This is a very secretive industry and hundreds of private social care providers are not providing proper care.

Social care providers will tell the potential "customers" that they offer "high quality care and value for money", but in reality there are thousands of residential care homes, nursing homes, and specialist homes, which are failing to look after the residents. There is a culture of neglect and a large number of homecare workers are guilty of carrying out violent actions against old people inside their homes. In the last three years 2015 to 2017, there were 23,000 incidents against the elderly, while they were at home and out of 23,000 incidents there were only 700 investigations and only 15 prosecutions. Every year more than 1,000 sick patients will die due to starvation and dehydration inside care homes and hospitals. Elderly hospital patients and care home residents are dying every day because they were neglected by care workers, doctors, and nurses. There are thousands of unnecessary and unexpected deaths in residential care homes, nursing homes, disability homes, specialist dementia homes, and local hospitals and the truth is being hidden. The general public are unaware of the desperate situation and thousands of UK pensioners have been abused and mistreated inside private care homes where their needs are being ignored. More than 100,00 vulnerable individuals are living in fear on a daily basis and 90% of social care workers and nurses have seen abuse taking place in care homes and nursing homes. People with dementia and alzheimer's disease and people with learning disabilities and mental health conditions require specialist care and they are being "targeted" by careless and abusive staff members who have a track record of assaulting vulnerable individuals. These people are not fit to work in the care industry because they are hostile towards people who need assistance and attention and there are thousands of incidents involving physical violence against residents being carried out by social care workers every year in the UK.

BUPA UK is supposed to provide specialist dementia care and it has 140 dementia homes in different areas around the UK. Unfortunately some of the staff members have been abusing vulnerable residents and patients and there are appalling conditions inside many BUPA care homes. There are hundreds of cases where dementia patients have been attacked and assaulted by careless nurses who are aggressive and there is widespread neglect taking place on a daily basis. The company directors receive around £700 million a year in profits and the "customers" are paying £1,200 a week. The family members and relatives are being deceived because in reality there are many BUPA specialist dementia care homes where the "specialists" are incompetent and they don't understand dementia issues. There are hundreds of private "premium care homes" where the "customers" are paying £1,500 a week and they are being abused by nurses who are hostile. The elderly population are being neglected and the conservative government has reduced local authority funding by 50%, while the company directors and owners of the big private care providers are receiving enormous salaries and "bonus payments" every year. Large numbers of care home residents are being overcharged by 60% or more and there is a nationwide shortage of "outstanding" care homes. The social care sector is collapsing and the situation is getting worse because the elderly population are developing complex health conditions and they will require specialist healthcare and expensive medical treatment.

In 2011, an elderly care home resident died due to death by scalding because the bath water was boiling hot and in 2012, an elderly care home resident with dementia died due to a fall because he was allowed to wander around in the middle of the night. The unfortunate individual fell through a first floor fire escape door to his death because he was allowed to open the fire door and the staff were not available to stop him. The man had a history of wandering around at night and opening doors and the care home did not provide any safeguarding or supervision. Old people with treatable health conditions are being denied medical treatment by staff members who have not been trained and in 2016, an elderly care home resident passed away because he was left in a critical condition by care home workers who couldn't be bothered to contact the doctor after a family member had raised concerns about her father's health and deteriorating condition. A family member noticed a deterioration due to kidney failure and the man had a history of kidney problems. The staff were informed and they agreed to arrange medical tests and call a doctor. 24 hours later the daughter received a phone call from the home to inform her of her father's death "due to natural causes". The staff failed to carry out medical tests and failed to notify the doctor on duty, the family members were told lies and in reality the unfortunate elderly resident endured unnecessary suffering, as well as being ignored by care home workers and care home supervisors because there is independent medical evidence to prove that the death was caused by kidney failure and could have been prevented.

Local authorities have cut social care funding levels to £2 per hour for each resident and thousands of UK pensioners are being ignored, while they are in a critical condition inside their homes and there is a complete lack of help and assistance. The majority of the elderly population cannot afford to pay the cost of social care and this is unacceptable in a rich country run by wealthy people. The GPs are failing elderly care home residents and there is a shortage of social services. Vulnerable individuals in care homes, nursing homes, and dementia homes are being ignored and they are becoming malnourished and dehydrated. The elderly are being forced to accept painful and invasive treatment, which is not in their best interests and against their wishes. The National Institute for Healthcare and Excellence (NICE) are guilty of ignorance and they need to take positive action, instead of talking. Private social care providers, hospital managers, mental health trusts, chief executives, company directors, and the millionaires who are controlling the social care industry are failing their local communities. UK pensioners are trapped inside hospital wards because the Department of Social Care has run out of money and this is creating a social care crisis. Private companies have made billions of pounds in profits, while thousands of nurses, carers, and medical staff who are under 25 are not receiving the minimum wage. In April 2018, the minimum wage was raised to £7.83 per hour for people over 25 and in 2019, it will rise again, but in reality people are being paid "a pittance" and they can't afford the cost of renting a flat. The system is unfair because social care workers, home care workers, and hospital nurses who are under 21 are being paid £5.90 per hour and if you work in customer services or computer technology, you can earn more than double the salary of a nurse or care worker. The environment within the NHS and the social care sector is tough and unpleasant and many people will choose an "easier life". Politics and profit have been given priority and the system is full of injustice.

New evidence is emerging revealing the truth about the corruption within big business corporations and global pharmaceutical giants. There are many cases of manslaughter by gross negligence taking place within the social care sector and the healthcare service. New independent medical research has found evidence of prescription drugs that have been contaminated, which are being given to people of all ages and the doctors and the psychiatrists have got a lot of important questions to answer. Families are being forced to fight against the system to make sure that the human rights of their loved ones are not violated. We have to change the culture of secrecy within the healthcare service and the social care industry. The hospital managers are forcing the doctors to abandon young people with mental health problems, people with learning disabilities, people with physical disabilities, people with dementia, and people with mental health conditions. When healthcare professionals are guilty of breaking the law, they are supposed to provide a proper explanation. Unfortunately the NHS is carrying out a widespread cover up and the higher managers and the chief executives have created a defence system and they are guilty of suppressing incriminating evidence of abuse, neglect, negligence, and manslaughter, which is happening on a daily basis inside many local hospitals and they are using "control and coercion" in order to silence the key witnesses. If the doctor has made an error of judgement and they are responsible for the unnecessary death of an elderly patient, they will try to make excuses and they will say that the death was caused by a "health condition" and due to "natural causes".

Some doctors are hiding the truth and people are being given large doses of harmful chemicals.

When a care home resident has passed away before their time due to neglect and negligence, there are a lot of managers who will refuse to admit that mistakes were made. There is evidence of widespread neglect inside care homes, disability homes, nursing homes, and specialist dementia homes. Agencies are sending nurses to work in care homes and hospitals and some of the nurses are responsible for causing the loss of life because they have not been trained. Nurses who have previous records of "failing to look after the elderly" are working in the social care industry and there are many incidents of nurses administering the wrong drugs, failing to notice when a person is having an allergic drug reaction, failing to notice when a person is dehydrated, and failing to notice when a person is deteriorating. The true numbers of old people who have been injured and the true numbers of preventable deaths have not been recorded and there are thousands of avoidable deaths inside residential social care homes, which have not been investigated. The care home managers have created a defence system and the staff members are not allowed to raise concerns when they see people being subjected to cruelty and abuse. Large numbers of social care workers and healthcare professionals are being forced to play a devious game, which is called "hide the facts" and the staff members are dismissed when they refuse to play the game. The solicitors and criminal barristers are receiving extortionate amounts of money for their services and the family members need to be prepared to stand up and speak out against injustice, if they want to find out the real truth. In reality social care workers, NHS doctors, NHS psychiatrists, psychiatric nurses, mental health clinicians, mental health nurses, hospital nurses, and GPs are mistreating far too many vulnerable individuals who need help and the national health service is suppressing the truth.

6

FAILURE OF THE DUTY OF CARE

The original foundations of the national health service were based upon the duty of care. Doctors, healthcare professionals, nurses, mental health nurses, and care workers are supposed to look after hospital patients and care home residents, but in reality the agenda has been given priority and the higher managers and chief executives have taken control of the system. When a person's needs are in conflict with the agenda, the health and safety of the individual will be sacrificed. The doctors and nurses are not allowed to use their intuition because they have to follow the rules created by higher managers. The hospital staff are being forced to carry out pointless medical procedures that are not in the patient's best interest. Individuals with critical conditions require urgent attention and the needs of the patient must be given priority. Local hospitals are required to provide a basic standard of care and good quality medical treatment and the doctors are supposed to create the patient's care plan. Unfortunately there are many cases where individuals with multiple health problems are not being assessed properly and they are not receiving the correct treatment because the doctors and the healthcare professionals are not aware of their medical history. The elderly are being given powerful drugs, which are not safe for people with complex health conditions. The psychiatrists and the clinicians are giving young people addictive anti-psychotic psychiatric drugs. Individuals with mental health conditions require "specialist treatment" and they are consuming noxious chemical compounds that cause damage to the brain cells and have a bad effect upon the patient's behaviour patterns. Psychiatric drugs can have a detrimental effect on the vital functions inside the physical body and the nurses are not able to give elderly mental health patients proper care because they don't understand the nature of mental health conditions. Many nurses are not being trained properly and there is a lack of compassion within the healthcare service and social care service.

When you are unwell and in need of help, you will have to visit a hospital and place your trust in a doctor. Many local hospitals are full of elderly wards where people are being neglected and the mental health wards and the psychiatric wards are full of people who have been abandoned by the system. Mental health patients and psychiatric patients are being forced to accept multiple injections of harmful chemicals and individuals who have been admitted into local hospitals for therapeutic treatment are being given large doses of toxic psychiatric drugs that don't work and they are being imprisoned. Toxic drugs can cause acute liver failure and when an elderly patient is taking medication, which is causing life life threatening side effects, they will need to be checked by the doctor immediately. In most cases, the doctors are unaware of the symptoms of side effects and they will carry on administering the drugs. If there aren't any family members available to speak out, the individual will continue to suffer and the nurses will continue the prescription. The doctors and the nurses are not fulfilling their duty of care and people are being treated with a lack of respect. Sometimes human lives are saved inside local hospitals and there are lucky people who have had treatment, which has extended their lifespan and they have been able to spend some time at home with their loved ones. Time is money and doctors, nurses, and healthcare staff are under extreme pressure and they cannot give the elderly the care that they need and there are many thousands of old people who have been forgotten by the healthcare service.

Millions of pounds have been spent on training doctors and nurses, but in reality they are being manipulated by the NHS managers who are dominating hospital healthcare. The daily time table has been given priority and the medical staff are being forced to work as quickly as possible. Good quality care takes a lot of time and there is a shortage of available time, which is causing unnecessary pain and suffering inside the hospital wards. Some patients will experience a reaction due to their medication and some patients will be able to tolerate their medication without any trouble. Consultant doctors and junior doctors are administering pharmaceutical drugs that hasten the death of elderly patients who are frail and this is against the law. When the doctors continue to prescribe toxic drugs that are causing serious health problems, they are guilty of negligence and they are carrying out abuse. People with mental health problems and people with psychiatric problems are not getting the help and therapy that they need. They are being treated like prisoners and they are being detained and held inside mental health wards and psychiatric wards when they are innocent. Paranoid individuals who are disturbed are having to wait for more than three months to be assessed and while they are waiting they will continue to suffer because the mental health services and the psychiatric services are failing to look after vulnerable individuals who are traumatised. The NHS is neglecting thousands of mental health patients, psychiatric patients, and dementia patients and the managers have wasted millions of pounds.

Care workers, nurses, and GPs are overworked and the elderly are being ignored inside care homes, nursing homes, and dementia homes. There are many staff members who have not been trained and they don't know how to carry out basic medical tests, as well as failing to check the medical history of patients and residents, there is a culture of neglect within the social care industry and the nurses are making basic mistakes on a daily basis because they are in a hurry. People are not being given enough food and water and some people are being given the wrong medicine. UK pensioners with complex mental health conditions and multiple health problems are being mistreated and in many cases, they are being misunderstood. Care home residents with dementia are taking far too many pharmaceutical drugs that contain dozens of harmful chemical agents. When all of the different toxic chemicals have been mixed together they have a detrimental effect upon the human body. This is completely unnecessary and it is happening because there is a nationwide lack of awareness within the social care industry. The government and the politicians are interfering with social care and they are wasting time because the big private providers are neglecting people every day inside care homes, nursing homes, and dementia homes and they are not providing any care.

If you sit inside a hospital ward for 12 hours from 10 am to 10 pm, you will see a familiar pattern of events taking place. The first thing that you notice is, there aren't any doctors inside the ward. They are supposed to create the care plan and make sure that people receive the correct treatment, while they are in hospital. When you are with a sick family member, you will have to wait for a long time before a doctor is available because they are busy working in the other departments inside the hospital. They don't have enough time to be able to get to know a person properly and check their medical history. Sometimes the doctors make mistakes and in many cases, they will refuse to admit that they have made an error. There are too many basic mistakes being made in hospitals due to human error and the nurses are unaware of the reality of complex health conditions. The nurses have to follow orders from the hospital managers and they have to visit a large number of hospital beds, carry out medical checks, and hand out prescription medicines, as well as trying to provide good quality care. Unfortunately there are thousands of nurses who are not able to provide any care and there are many problems with recruiting new nurses because they are being paid a minimum wage. Thousands of nurses who work in the social care sector are being paid less than £7 per hour and they are neglecting people who need help. The doctors and the healthcare professionals are not looking after people properly and the national health service and the big private social care providers are failing to provide any care. There are thousands of vulnerable individuals who are being forgotten and there is widespread chaos within the system.

The doctors and the nurses are being forced to carry out pointless medical procedures that cause physical injury and the higher managers have taken control of the system. There is a selfish attitude within NHS management and some managers and executives only care about "power and money". Modern healthcare is too complicated and precious time is being wasted. People are being subjected to cruelty inside the elderly wards, mental health wards, and the psychiatric wards and some of the staff members are carrying out abuse. Doctors and nurses are carrying out unnecessary medical treatments inside the elderly wards on a daily basis. Mental health patients and psychiatric patients are being given powerful drugs, instead of therapy and some of the drugs are harmful. There is a massive shortage of financial resources available for mental healthcare and psychiatric care due to the lack of investment and there are large numbers of mental health staff and psychiatric staff who need more training because they don't know how to help people. The elderly are being forced to accept poor quality healthcare and in many cases, the consultant doctors are unaware of their medical history and condition. Old people are losing weight inside the hospital wards because they are not eating enough food. The elderly are being given unsafe drugs that contain toxic chemical agents and individuals with terminal conditions are not receiving "end of life" care.

Most hospitals are overcrowded and there aren't enough beds. There are thousands of UK pensioners inside the elderly wards who should be at home and there are people who are being mistreated inside the elderly wards. Vulnerable individuals are being neglected and this is unacceptable. People are becoming dehydrated and they are losing weight, some people are having trouble sleeping because the hospital beds are so uncomfortable and there is too much "noise" in the wards during the night time hours. Individuals who are frail and weak are being forgotten and their health is deteriorating because they have developed multiple bacterial infections. Some of the medical staff are not using their common sense and there is a lack of basic intelligence inside many local hospitals. Old people with common diseases are not receiving any care and old people with terminal respiratory conditions are being given a breakfast meal consisting of mashed potato with sausage and gravy, which is impossible for them to eat. The "end of life" care provided by local hospitals is not fit for purpose and the junior doctors are being left in charge of critically ill patients without any supervision from the consultant doctors. When it is time to administer the "end of life" injection, 99% of junior doctors will avoid telling the truth because they don't want to upset the family members. In many cases, they will say: "we are going to give your loved one a sedative to make them feel comfortable", but in reality the person will pass away within a few hours. If the family members decide to take a break away from the bedside, they will not be there when their loved one passes away. The truth is coming out and the NHS is failing the elderly population because the duty of care is not being fulfilled by the medical staff inside many local hospitals across the UK.

Thousands of hospital wards are out of date and in desperate need of investment and old people are not receiving any care. Most hospital wards are too small and the beds are too close to each other. Dignity and privacy have been sacrificed and elderly patients are being abused in front of other patients and their visitors. There is a complete lack of therapeutic treatment and people are being subjected to medical treatments, which are harmful and against the wishes of the family members. There are many elderly wards where people are not safe and UK pensioners who paid a lot of tax during their lifetime are being imprisoned inside NHS hospitals. UK citizens with complicated health conditions are not receiving the care and attention that they need because the consultant doctors are too busy. Elderly patients, mental health patients, and psychiatric patients are being treated like "second class citizens" and they are forced to endure harsh discrimination and physical violence. There are hundreds of pharmaceutical drugs, which have detrimental effects on the human body. Consultant doctors and clinical psychiatrists have placed their trust in the pharmaceutical industry, but in reality the global drug giants are producing "medicines for profit". A large number of prescription drugs are toxic and NHS consultant doctors, NHS psychiatrists, and NHS mental health clinicians are not providing safe healthcare. The family members need to take control of the situation and take their loved ones home where they belong.

Healthcare services and social care services are treating hospital patients and care home residents like "numbers", instead of human beings. Doctors, nurses, and care workers are being forced to carry out "the plan" created by the private providers. The hospitals are in crisis and the social care sector is collapsing due to the lack of funding and too much profit taking. There are millions of people who need help and support and there are many situations where good care is not available. In reality the elderly are being subjected to unnecessary suffering and extreme pain, while they are in agony. UK citizens are being subjected to cruelty and their human rights are being violated across the country. The time has come for individuals to change the system and make sure they receive fair treatment and safe medicines. When a person is experiencing a drug reaction, the family will have to confront the doctors and the nurses to get the prescription stopped because the healthcare professionals will refuse to admit that the drugs are causing a problem. When a sick patient is close to death and they still have an appetite, they will need liquid nutrition containing protein, multi-vitamins, and essential minerals. Individuals who cannot swallow solid food are being given cooked meals, which they cannot eat and this is a total waste of money. The hospitals provide glucose and saline fluid replacement, but they don't provide any liquid nutrition. There are disturbing numbers of the elderly population who are starving inside the elderly wards because they can't eat solid food and the nurses are not providing proper care. Thousands of UK pensioners are also suffering due to dehydration and there are a lot of patients with terminal diseases who are isolated and distressed.

Human beings are not machines and we are being forced to accept a healthcare service and a social care service, which is based upon following an agenda. People are being "processed" by the system and they are not receiving any care. Doctors, nurses, medical staff, mental health clinicians, psychiatrists, and care workers are supposed to follow the care plan, but in reality they are mistreating thousands of UK citizens every day. There is a total lack of care and the social services are not looking after disabled patients, mental health patients, psychiatric patients, and old people who require specialist care. The social care industry is being dominated by the big private providers and they are not looking after many thousands of care home residents. There are many small private providers who are guilty of employing staff who have not been given any training and some staff are causing physical injury because they don't know how to handle a frail elderly person. Individuals are not being treated with respect and they are being abused inside care homes, nursing homes, and dementia homes and they are not being supervised properly. Residents who require 24 hour care are being left on their own for long periods of time when they are in pain because the staff members are unavailable and this is happening on a daily basis because selfish people are running the system and they are taking control.

This is the "sad reality" throughout the UK and it is time for change. The people at the top have interfered with healthcare and social care and they have created poor quality health systems and hazardous social systems. The main priorities are: reaching targets, forcing the staff to follow pointless rules and stupid regulations, taking away freedom, and the creation of a prescription drug market full of poor quality medicines, which are dangerous. Poisonous medicines are harmful and they should be banned. The doctors need to stand up and speak out and tell the truth. The people who work in healthcare and social care who are careless and selfish are giving the staff members who work hard a bad name. The majority of hospital nurses and care workers are not able to provide any care because they are carrying out the agenda and have not been trained properly. There is a funding crisis within the NHS and the managers are spending too much money on expensive advertising, while individuals who need help are being ignored. The annual cost of prescriptions for type 2 diabetes has reached £1 billion and millions of UK citizens are being given the wrong dietary advice and patients are not cutting down their carbohydrate/saturated fat intake in order to reduce their blood sugar levels. The concept of socialism and shared wealth within our society hasn't worked and the healthcare industry and the social care industry are like a giant tower, which is falling down and underneath the debris, there are many thousands of victims who lost their lives because they were abandoned. The family members who decide to entrust the system with the precious lives of their elderly loved ones, are making a big mistake. Consultant surgeons are carrying out unnecessary operations and consultant doctors are prescribing toxic drugs. If you are an elderly person and you have a low priority disease and a heart condition, you will be neglected inside the local acute medical ward. Thousands of hospital patients and care home residents are suffering everyday in isolation and the national health service and the private providers are guilty of a massive nationwide failure of the duty of care.

7

DANGEROUS DOCTORS

Some doctors wear white uniforms and they wear white because it is pure and it represents wisdom and knowledge. White is a neutral colour and it does not contain any other colours. Doctors and healers have been wearing white for thousands of years and it is part of ancient human history, unfortunately the majority of UK doctors are working in grey areas and sometimes they make mistakes and errors of judgement. The doctors are not aware of the dangers of prescription medicines and there are too many mistakes happening inside the elderly wards, mental health wards, psychiatric wards, and the GP surgeries. People are receiving poor quality medical treatment and in many cases, they are being given an incorrect diagnosis and drugs, which do not have any health benefits. There is a lack of care in the hospital wards and the doctors are absent for most of the time. Consultant hospital doctors are in a position of power and authority and they have access to advanced technology available for patient diagnosis and treatment. They are supposed to be guardians of the healthcare service and we place our trust in them and expect them to do their best when we are sick and in need of help. It takes at least 13 years to become a consultant doctor and it costs £500,000 to train a consultant hospital doctor. It takes at least 10 years to become a GP and it costs £250,000 to train a GP. Millions of pounds have been invested in training and all of the doctors have to complete the 5 year medical degree course in a medical university, including the 2 year foundation programme, which includes further training and work experience.

Trainee doctors are not allowed to use their intuition because they have to follow "clinical training" in order to receive "professional status", and in reality there are far too many dangerous doctors who work in the NHS and many GPs have not been trained properly. There are around 7,500 general practice surgeries and the standard of care is deteriorating within general practice. The General Medical Council (GMC) are incompetent and they are covering up the failures of locum doctors who have made medical errors and the hospital managers are incompetent and they are covering up the failures of consultant doctors who are failing to look after people. There are many locum doctors from foreign countries working in the UK. A large number of foreign locums have been found guilty of misconduct and medical negligence. Lethal locum doctors are being allowed to work in local hospitals and they are being ignored by the GMC. The bad doctors are hiding their past history of patient abuse and they are continuing to work in the healthcare service. The system has become careless and people are not treated with respect. There are a lot of problems with the standard of care and treatment of elderly patients, psychiatric patients, and young patients with mental health conditions and disabilities. The healthcare system and the social care industry are in desperate need of improvement and there is a crisis in healthcare funding and social care funding for the elderly population.

GPs, hospital doctors, clinicians, and psychiatrists spend too much time filling out forms and there is too much paperwork and thousands of NHS professionals are failing to provide therapeutic healthcare. Old people in hospitals and care homes are being left alone when they are in pain and this is happening across the country on a daily basis. Local hospitals and care homes are not providing proper safeguarding and large numbers of hospital patients and care home residents have lost their lives, due to an accident that could have been avoided if the staff members had been with the victim. There is a total lack of doctors in the hospitals at weekends and this is a problem if you happen to be sick or have an accident at home on Saturday or Sunday. The consultant doctors are absent from the wards and the NHS is using large numbers of locum doctors and there are around 8,500 locum doctors working inside the local hospitals. There are more than 100,000 job vacancies within the national health service and the numbers are rising. The number of locums working in the UK is rising and some of the employment agencies are making profits by supplying locum doctors who have a track record of carrying out abuse. Local hospitals are failing to raise concerns about the bad locums because they think that the doctors will sue the national health service. Some of the locums are guilty of manslaughter and the hospital managers are hiding the truth. Hundreds of foreign locum doctors who work in local hospitals have been found guilty of misconduct in their home countries and some of the locums have not been trained properly. In the last 10 years during 2008 to 2018, there were more than 10,000 reported cases of negligence and neglect and thousands of incidents have not been reported because the victims are seriously ill and they cannot communicate properly. In reality there are thousands of patients who are being put at risk every day.

Negligent doctors are being allowed to work in the NHS and the General Medical Council (GMC) has been protecting them from prosecution by destroying the medical records and the past history of guilty doctors. Some of the doctors are from the UK and the other doctors are from foreign countries. The British Medical Association (BMA) is full of arrogance and it has become like an elite society of doctors and professionals who are rich and wealthy and are not able to relate to an ordinary person because they don't understand the circumstances of "common people". The GPs are being paid too much money and in many cases, they can't help people and they are providing poor quality healthcare. The general practise system is outdated and it is not fit for purpose. Some GPs are prescribing anti-depressants and tranquilizers for more than 10 years and this is not in the person's best interest because anxious individuals are becoming addicted to their medication. Consultant doctors have got an enormous amount of clinical knowledge and detailed information about the structure of the human body, but in reality there are large numbers of doctors who don't understand hepatotoxicity and they don't recognise the symptoms of an allergic/hypersensitive reaction caused by prescription drugs. When you are with an elderly family member and they are experiencing a drug reaction, it is very hard to get the prescription stopped. Most consultant doctors are unavailable because they are too busy and you are forced to see the junior doctor, who will tell you that the symptoms are caused by the individual's health condition. A lot of junior doctors are not telling the truth and this sorry situation is repeating itself inside hospital wards, mental health wards, and psychiatric wards on a regular basis and in reality thousands of UK pensioners in local hospitals are deteriorating every day and they are not receiving any healthcare.

Foreign doctors who are guilty of causing the death of their patients are being allowed to work inside local hospitals. Doctor Hourmann from Argentina moved to the UK in 2006, after facing a manslaughter charge in Spain during 2005. He worked in the NHS from 2006 to 2010, and he was found guilty of manslaughter in 2010. Doctor Neale from Canada moved to the UK in 1986, and he was found guilty of manslaughter in Canada in 1985. He worked in the NHS from 1986 to 1995, and he was found guilty of 33 cases of medical negligence in the UK during 1987 to 1995. Some of the victims he operated on received life changing injuries and they were subjected to painful and harmful surgery and they were given dangerous treatments, which they did not need. Doctor Sartori from Austria moved to the UK in 1995. He worked in the NHS from 1995 to 2008. In 2005, he was found guilty of 4 cases of manslaughter in Australia. He gave the victims an "alternative cancer therapy", which involved administering lethal injections containing industrial solvents and paint strippers. The unfortunate individuals died from blood poisoning and the coroner said that they were subjected to torture and a painful death. The doctors were given a valid licence to practice in the UK and all of the doctors had a past history of patient abuse in other countries. The GMC is protecting guilty doctors and this is unacceptable and in reality a medical licence to practice can also be used as a licence to carry out illegal euthanasia.

The government has said that it will take action to remove the bad doctors from the register and doctors who have a record of causing injury will be struck off the British Medical Register and banned from working in the UK, but unfortunately this is not happening because the Medical Practitioners Tribunal Service (MPTS) is giving guilty doctors the freedom to work in the NHS and elderly hospital patients are in peril. In 2017, hundreds of doctors were struck off the list and 75% were from foreign counties. There is a nationwide problem with doctors who have not been given enough training in their home countries and many foreign doctors are being trained by health schools and medical schools, which are not being run properly. The global medical industry is full of fake schools and corrupt companies. During 2010 to 2015, there were 460 negligent doctors who were banned from practicing. More than 330 doctors were from foreign countries and the UK has got a big problem with incompetent doctors. The reason why 75% of the doctors being struck off are foreign, is because the UK doctors know how to hide their mistakes. Bad doctors are good at telling lies and they are refusing to admit their past history of misconduct, this is why there are fewer British doctors being struck off the register. The medical establishment is trying to put all of the blame onto foreign doctors and they are not telling the truth. In reality the GMC are protecting guilty British doctors and guilty locum doctors and thousands of vulnerable individuals have received life long injuries.

An independent report has revealed evidence of widespread negligence within local hospitals and local GP surgeries. According to the report, a large number of hospital tests are harmful and unnecessary and they are a waste of money. The GPs are not providing safe healthcare and there is too much medicine and too much treatment. The government is forcing doctors to treat more people and the GPs are giving people drugs for minor health conditions that will never cause them any harm or pain. Healthy individuals are being admitted into hospitals for surgery and medical tests, which are not necessary. People are not given any information about the dangers of medical tests and hospital treatments and there are many treatments, which do not have any health benefits and are dangerous. Millions of UK citizens are being put at risk by having surgery and pills that they don't need and the GPs are prescribing too many unnecessary drugs. The hospitals and the doctors are carrying out large scale misdiagnosis and the "overtreatment" of thousands of patients and this is happening every day. People are being given an incorrect diagnosis and medical treatment and drugs, which are causing health problems. There is a culture of "more is better" and the doctors are under too much pressure to take action, there are many situations where the person does not need any tests or drugs or surgery and the best option is to do nothing at all. Unfortunately thousands of UK citizens are being diagnosed with conditions that will never cause any symptoms or deterioration in their health and they are taking unsafe drugs and they are being subjected to harmful medical treatments and painful surgery. In the majority of cases, the unfortunate individual will experience a detrimental effect on their health. In reality the hospital doctors and hospital surgeons are causing a lot of needless suffering and pain and there are many thousands of elderly victims who have had a traumatic experience.

Hospital healthcare is based on a financial reward payment system created by the higher managers and the government. The doctors are paid when the patient receives a diagnosis and medical treatment, the doctors are not being paid for the amount of successful treatments, they are being paid for the amount of people who receive prescriptions and millions of UK citizens are being given drugs for no reason. When a person visits their local surgery for a consultation appointment, there are many situations where doing nothing is the best option. Unfortunately most GPs will try to take action and they will try to persuade the "customer" to accept drugs and hospital treatment, which are not in the person's best interest. The GPs and the hospital doctors are not providing proper healthcare and people are being ignored and neglected on a daily basis. The medical schools and medical universities are training the doctors to take action, instead of taking the time to find the best possible solution. There is a problem within medical culture and doctors are not using their intuition because they are overworked and they cannot think clearly. Doctors and surgeons are being paid to carry out useless tests and medical treatments for no reason, which are a massive waste of resources and have no health benefits, as well as needless invasive surgery, which is painful and harmful. Doctors are being paid to prescribe toxic drugs that have severe side effects and are addictive. When a person visits a GP and they have "mental health problems" most GPs will prescribe drugs, instead of therapy because if they do nothing, they will not be paid any money. The current situation is shameful and things have got to change. In reality there are many thousands of individuals with chronic anxiety who are suffering every day because healthcare professionals, mental health clinicians, and psychiatrists are giving people drugs, which cause "mental health problems".

Senior doctors have started a campaign to stop the GPs who are prescribing unnecessary drugs, as well as sending people to hospitals for tests, treatment, and surgery, which are not necessary. Junior GP doctors are prescribing large doses of pills for mild depression, type 2 diabetes, and high blood pressure and there are too many blood tests being carried out in the local hospitals around the country. There are many people who need therapy and they are being mistreated by the doctors who are being put under pressure to give people drugs, instead of providing therapeutic treatment. Junior hospital doctors are overworked and they are under extreme pressure and some of them are committing suicide. Independent records show that 1,200 GPs are being treated by the mental health service and there are 1.5 million UK citizens who are addicted to tranquilizers. During 2018, the local pharmacies will hand out more than 10 million benzodiazepine prescriptions for anxiety and the numbers of addicts are rising on a daily basis. There is evidence to prove that the drugs, which are being used to treat anxiety, depression, attention deficit disorder, and dementia are responsible for more than 500,000 deaths in the western world every year and the doctors are not being honest with people regarding the dangers of prescription drugs and medicines. A large number of anti-depressant drugs and dementia drugs are ineffective and they are a waste of money. The GPs are prescribing anti-depressants and tranquilizers that damage the central nervous system and are not in the person's best interest. UK health experts have issued warnings to the doctors because they are handing out too many prescriptions and there is proof of the damage that is caused by the long term use of tranquilizers containing benzodiazepines and valium.

In 2011, there were a number of cases against GP doctors who continued to prescribe valium, which is harmful for more than ten years. Valium tranquilizers are being used to treat anxiety and chronic stress and the doctors are prescribing them for many years, while the patients are continuing to deteriorate. The drugs are supposed to be used as a short term treatment no longer than six months and they are not suitable for long term use because they cause drug addiction. There is a lot of evidence of benzodiazepines causing brain damage. UK lawyers have reported a rapid rise in the amount of criminal cases of medical negligence. People are taking legal action against the GPs after they became addicted to valium and the doctors are guilty because they continued the prescription of drugs, which are addictive. The long term use of valium causes "drug dependency", the withdrawal process can cause physical symptoms, which are extremely painful and worse than the original condition. Hundreds of long term drug addicts were taken off the drugs too quickly, leaving them disabled and in agony and many people were left with lifelong injuries and painful health conditions. Coming off tranquilizers too quickly can cause seizures and loss of life and thousands of prescription drug addicts are being subjected to a rapid detoxification programme, which is unsafe and they are in danger. The NHS financial payment system has led to poor quality treatment and there are many thousands of cases of "overtreatment" being carried out inside the hospital wards and the GP surgeries every year. The Royal College of GPs is in denial about this problem because they fear prosecution. In reality there are intelligent doctors and sometimes they save human life. Unfortunately there are large numbers of junior doctors and consultant doctors who are not looking after people properly and they are working in the healthcare service. When you trust your intuition you will find new knowledge. When you use toxic drugs you will make serious mistakes and vulnerable individuals will die before their time and inside local hospitals, mental health hospitals, and psychiatric hospitals there are some dangerous doctors.

8

POISONOUS MEDICINE

We have a big problem in the healthcare industry and in the social care industry, which is also happening in many other global industries. Harmful chemicals have been added to the medicines and they also contain artificial additives, which are unsafe. A lot of money has been spent on testing prescription medicines and detailed scientific research is carried out to make sure the medicines are safe and effective. Unfortunately this has not stopped thousands of toxic drugs being released into the global healthcare system and these medicines are being given to the general public by doctors, psychiatrists, mental health nurses, GPs, and care workers. The science and technology involved in the development and testing of modern medicines is supposed to protect the patient from harm, but in reality the pharmaceutical companies are producing large numbers of dangerous prescription drugs and they are being run by a small group of extremely wealthy people. When you have a lot of money, it is very easy to break the law and the big private drug companies do not care about human suffering because they are making enormous profits.

If you go into a beef burger shop, you can buy a fast cheap dinner for less than £5, but if you keep on buying the same meal every day, week after week, month after month, you are going to become very ill. This is exactly the same as taking poisonous medicine and the health of the physical body will be seriously damaged by the toxins in the food. The pharmaceutical giants have created a mass produced consumer market for drugs and society is the "customer". In reality vulnerable patients are being used like a financial resource to feed the corrupt drug industry run by selfish and greedy people. There are some lucky people who are alive because they received an extension of their lifespan by taking certain medicines, but unfortunately there are large numbers of hospital patients, mental health patients, psychiatric patients, GP patients, and elderly care home residents who experienced detrimental effects on their health caused by prescription drugs. Some medicines are safe and some medicines are harmful and we live in a world where there are hundreds of synthetic drugs, which are unsafe. The global pharmaceutical drug industry has caused millions of needless deaths around the world and there are millions of innocent victims in different countries who have passed away before their time. The drug industry is developing new medicines based upon corrosive acids and harmful chemicals and the medicines have been contaminated. The medicines inside plants and natural compounds that exist in nature are based upon molecular chains and most of the medicines are pure and safe for human consumption. The drug industry is spending billions and they are creating "expensive poisons", which are not medicines. The scientists are changing the atomic structure of natural compounds and they are creating synthetic substances, which are used to produce the medicines. The key to this process is very simple, the scientists who are working in the company laboratories are breaking the molecular chains, which are found inside the natural elements. The drug companies have "broken the chain" and they have distorted and destroyed the blueprint of the DNA that exists within nature and the universe. Private companies are making massive profits and they are releasing industrial grade chemicals into the global healthcare system. The doctors, nurses, mental health clinicians, psychiatrists, care workers, and the GPs are giving people drugs, which cause blindness, hepatitis, and brain damage.

Poisonous medicines can cause toxic shock. When a person has toxic shock, they will experience a violent physical reaction due to the chemical agents within the medicine. There are hundreds of severe side effects, which are caused by medicines that contain poisons and here is a list of some of the symptoms: nausea, vomiting, slurred speech, dizziness, seizures, nerve damage, skin damage, water retention, blurred vision, loss of vision, confusion, disorientation, hallucination, rapid breathing, rapid heart rate, muscle wasting, muscle weakness, bone damage, memory loss, weight loss, dehydration, exhaustion, loss of appetite, high blood pressure, jaundice, blood poisoning, chronic hepatitis, renal failure, chronic liver damage, liver failure, and heart failure. UK healthcare regulators are supposed to protect the NHS patients and they are allowing the release of millions of toxic tablets into the healthcare service and the healthcare professionals are administering harmful medicines on a daily basis. Clinical trials are required by the law in order to test new medicines to make sure that they are effective. Small groups of sick people volunteer and they are given a dose of the new medicine, which is being tested. Unfortunately large corrupt private drug companies have been carrying out secret clinical trials and medical tests, which have not been approved by the regulators and this is illegal. When a person's death has been caused by antibiotic drugs it raises concerns about the safety of the drugs being prescribed. If the family members are brave enough to complain, the hospital will be forced to carry out an internal investigation into the circumstances and we have a disturbing nationwide problem because the consultant doctors are not telling the truth and they will refuse to admit that they are giving people poisonous medicine. The chief executive will say that "the person's death was caused by their health condition and they died of natural causes", but in reality this is the "standard official statement" that the hospitals repeat to the family members when a loved one has passed away prematurely because they were given too many unsafe drugs.

Consultant doctors, mental health clinicians, psychiatrists, and GPs are handing out medicines that damage the brain cell network. Millions of UK citizens are being given noxious chemicals and large numbers of healthcare workers are giving the patients too many drugs. Neurotoxicity is a medical term referring to "the poisonous effects of harmful substances inside the human brain and central nervous system". Neurotoxic drugs can cause and illness and sickness. We have a hidden epidemic within our society and there are neurotoxins inside processed supermarket foods, consumer products, building products, commercial industries, farming products, herbicides, pesticides, beauty products, and pharmacy products. There are many independent neuro-toxicologists who study the effects of medical drugs and the new research evidence is shocking and disturbing. Prescription drug poisoning can often be the cause of a mental illness and prescription drug induced neurotoxicity can cause many different types of neurological conditions, as well as numerous psychological and psychiatric disorders. There is a lot evidence confirming the link between drug induced neurotoxicity and brain damage and the symptoms include problems with: memory, concentration, reaction time, sleeping, thinking, anxiety and depression, confusion, personality changes, circulation problems, and fatigue. Some drugs can cause permanent damage and serious injury to the major organs due to the artificial man made compounds.

Neurotoxins and corrosive acids are being given to anxious young patients and frail elderly patients and this is an abuse of the individual's human rights. Neurotoxins are poisons that destroy the nerve tissues and they can cause damage to the blood/brain barrier, which protects the brain from poisons. The poisons also destroy vital nerves and neurons inside the brain and they damage the functions of the human central nervous system. People are having to endure extremely unpleasant side effects due to the total lack of understanding within the general medical establishment regarding neurotoxicity. Here are some of the different neurotoxic drugs that are being prescribed by UK doctors: antibiotics, anti-depressants, anti-psychotics, prozac, psychiatric drugs, tranquilizers, sleeping pills, drugs for attention deficit disorder, drugs for thought disorders, and drugs for anxiety. All of these medications are designed for short term use no longer than six months, but in reality the doctors are continuing to hand out prescriptions that are harmful for many years. Consultant doctors, healthcare professionals, mental health clinicians, psychiatrists, nurses, care workers, and GPs are failing to recognise the side effects and they are failing to provide a proper diagnosis. Neurotoxic drugs can cause damage to the human brain leading to violent and hostile behaviour, agitation, hyper-mania, dementia, multiple personality disorders, alzheimer's disease, parkinson's disease, suicide, psychosis, schizophrenia, depression, and paralysis of the physical body. Individuals with psychiatric conditions are "drugged up" with toxic anti-psychotics and there is a complete lack of clinical knowledge because the doctors have not been given any toxicology training. The elderly are being subjected to unnecessary suffering and physical injury caused by pointless medical treatment and the hospital nurses are failing to recognise the condition of elderly patients. The situation has to change because there are too many needless premature deaths inside the local hospitals every year caused by "drug induced neurotoxicity" and the doctors are failing to recognise the signs of brain damage.

The solution to this massive problem is simple. We have to invest more money into independent scientific medical research. Independent scientists and independent doctors have discovered new knowledge. Some modern medicines destroy the immune system and the liver and some medicines can cause numerous mental health conditions. Mainstream medicine and mainstream science are narrow minded and dogmatic because they don't accept the ancient wisdom and higher knowledge. Independent medicine is based upon intuition and common sense, unfortunately there is absence of intelligence within social care homes and local hospitals. The NHS is prescribing a dangerous antibiotic medicine for tuberculosis patients and it contains three different chemical agents mixed together. The agents are isoniazid, rifampicin, and pyrazinamide. These chemicals are corrosive and they destroy the vital enzymes inside the liver, as well as the healthy bacteria inside the stomach. The chemicals also destroy large numbers of healthy cells and they cause damage inside the physical body. The medicine is called Rifater and it can cause acute liver failure and the side effects are extremely severe. If you pour sulphuric acid on your skin, you will receive a sharp pain as the acid dissolves the skin cells. Some antibiotic medicines contain corrosive acids and chemical agents that destroy the soft tissues and membranes within the major organs and these drugs are unsafe. The consultant doctors, mental health clinicians, psychiatrists, and the GPs are giving people substances that damage the vital functions within the human brain and they are failing in their duty of care.

Healthcare professionals are trying to cure common diseases by using synthetic drugs and this is impossible because you cannot ignore the human immune system. This is how the human body fights infection and disease. Artificial man made drugs will never work as well as the auto-immune system and this is a fact of life. Pharmaceutical drugs contain many unnatural substances and chemical agents, which have been added to the medicines. Mother nature provides all of the elements, compounds, medicinal trees, and plants that can cure all of our diseases and new medicines need to be developed to boost the immune system. Some independent doctors have developed new medical treatments and they have discovered new medicines, which are being used in the UK. The national health service and the medical establishment are trying to stop new treatments and new medicines because they are being controlled by the drug industry and they are taking away the freedom to choose safe medicine. The doctors and the healthcare professionals are supposed to help people by giving them advice and guidance, but unfortunately thousands of vulnerable individuals are being forced to accept invasive treatment, which is not in their best interest and unnecessary drugs that cause life threatening health problems. UK citizens who have placed their trust in a doctor are being asked to place their trust in medicines that have been created and produced by "suspicious pharmaceutical scientists" inside a private laboratory in a foreign country. The men and women who are wearing the white uniforms are supposed to have the best interests of society as their main priority, but in reality the truth is coming out and there is no doubt, you cannot trust the global drug industry.

The elderly are taking expensive drugs, which are having a bad effect on their health and the doctors have decided to ignore the dangers and they are making mistakes. There is a grey area here and large numbers of UK doctors are "living in a bubble" and they are unaware of reality because they will continue to prescribe "harmful medicines" for sick patients and there is evidence of the damage caused by synthetic drugs administered by hospital doctors, psychiatrists, GPs, and care workers. In the tribal communities where there are ancient traditions, the village medicine man or medicine woman will have taken all of the natural medicines, which they will use to treat a sick person and this is an important part of shamanic training and education. There are plants that contain deadly toxins and the shamans need to know that all of their medicines are safe and harmless. NHS professionals have received expensive medical training, unfortunately they are guilty of failing to recognise the symptoms of an allergic reaction caused by prescription drugs. In the majority of cases, they will continue to administer the drugs and the unfortunate individual will pass away before their time. This is happening on a regular basis inside hospitals, mental health wards, psychiatric wards, and private care homes. The symptoms of side effects caused by toxic drugs are much more serious than symptoms caused by most common diseases. People are not being told the whole truth about the potential risks of medical treatments and they are being mistreated by the healthcare professionals and medical staff.

Private drug companies provide a lot of detailed information about their medicines and the doctors are ignoring the warnings because they trust the drug industry. The global drug companies are aware of the fact that most of their medicines are unsafe and they have to provide guidelines for doctors and healthcare professionals to follow. The industry is spending millions fighting against the families of the victims who have passed away and there are hundreds of UK legal cases because the families are fighting to get compensation for the abuse that they have suffered. People need to wake up and realize that they are being poisoned by the pharmaceutical corporations and the big commercial companies who sell consumer products containing toxins and poisons. Society is becoming a prisoner within a conspiracy of authorities and most people don't know who to trust. Hospital patients, mental health patients, psychiatric patients, disabled patients, patients who have learning disabilities, patients with attention deficit disorder, and GP patients are being denied access to new medicines because the healthcare service is refusing to pay the extra money. Millions of people are being given prescription drugs that cause health problems. Some people are being given antibiotics for minor health conditions and they are receiving a health benefit and there are some antibiotic drugs that can save a human life in situations where the person has a bacterial infection, but there are also some harmful antibiotic drugs, which are being prescribed for people with common respiratory diseases.

Multinational global corporations are creating mass produced medical products for the consumer health market and most of their products have been contaminated due to the industrial grade chemical agents and noxious synthetic substances, which have been added to the fake medicines. The acid test for a real medicine is based upon a simple philosophy. It should not injure or kill human life and it should do more good than harm. If a new drug has got a long complicated scientific name, it doesn't mean that it is safe. In the majority of cases, longer names mean stronger poisons contained within the drugs. The UK regulators have not been able to stop deadly medicines being released into the national health service. The consultant doctors, junior doctors, mental health clinicians, psychiatrists, and the GPs are not telling the truth and UK citizens are being given harmful drugs for too long because there is a total lack of care within the system. If you have never taken toxic drugs, you cannot know what it feels like to be poisoned and the doctors are not aware of the symptoms of a violent allergic/hypersensitive drug reaction because they have not had any toxicology training. The medical schools and medical universities are training doctors to carry out "the plan", which is being controlled by the "private medical industry". In reality the needs of people who require help are being ignored on a daily basis inside the elderly wards, mental health wards, psychiatric wards, care homes, nursing homes, dementia homes, and specialist homes. A large number of families have seen their loved ones suffering in a hospital bed because the doctors are administering toxic drugs. When an individual is in this situation, the family members need to speak out and take control and stop the administration of unsafe drugs. Consultant doctors, mental health clinicians, NHS psychiatrists, and GPs need to wake up because they are prescribing large doses of poisonous medicine.

9

THE WARDS OF HORROR

Home is where the heart is and individuals who require homecare are being ignored. Large numbers of the elderly population are being admitted into local hospitals across the country against their wishes. Some people have received good quality care in a hospital ward and they are the lucky ones. Far too many sick patients are being neglected inside the elderly wards, mental health wards, and psychiatric wards and they are receiving poor quality healthcare. The elderly wards are full of people who are not being looked after and old people are not receiving the care and attention that they need. This is happening on a daily basis and the medical staff are not able to provide any care because they are too busy. The hospitals have got too many different departments and they don't work together and there is a lack of organisation in the wards. Inside an NHS hospital there are intensive care wards, acute medical wards, isolation wards, specialist wards, and elderly wards. Some of the individuals in the elderly wards are in a critical condition, they require specialist care and need to be taken to the intensive care wards where they can receive special care and attention, but in reality critically ill patients are being failed and they are being sent to the elderly wards because the intensive care wards are overcrowded and full up.

Old people who need special care are suffering because there is a massive shortage of resources. Valuable time is being wasted, there is a lack of proper care and UK pensioners are being left alone when they are in pain. Elderly patients, mental health patients, and psychiatric patients are being subjected to cruel treatment inside chaotic wards and the hospitals are not providing any safeguarding.

Individuals with common respiratory diseases are slipping through the "care system net" and they are being abandoned by the doctors. The national health service is supposed to protect vulnerable individuals from harm and it is failing to look after old people and the nurses are supposed to look after the patients and administer life saving drugs, but in reality the majority of hospital wards are not providing any care and the elderly are being left alone, while they are deteriorating and the nurses are unaware of the situation. Medical staff are making too many basic errors and this is happening on a daily basis. When you are in a hurry you will forget things and when you are in a rush you will make errors and mistakes. Doctors and nurses are being forced to carry out harmful medical treatments and in many cases, they are not able to provide any care. There are a lot of problems with recruiting new nurses and the nursing agencies are supplying nurses to cover the shortages. Some nursing agencies are sending careless nurses to work in the hospital wards and they are failing to protect the hospitals from staff members who have been found guilty of negligence and misconduct.

The British Nursing Agency is sending out large numbers of incompetent nurses who are working inside the hospital wards and there are disturbing problems with some locum nurses. Locum nurses who have a track record of carrying out abuse are being allowed to work in local hospitals and they are ignoring old people who are in pain and some patients are being given the wrong medicine. The locums are also failing to check the medical records, medical notes, and past history of their patients. Some of the locum nurses are hostile and aggressive towards individuals who are distressed and the bad locums are bullying the patients because they cannot be bothered to look after them. There is a culture of neglect and some of the locums are careless and lazy. The health and safety of UK citizens has been sacrificed and old people are being put at risk inside local hospitals. Trainee junior doctors are being left in charge of individuals who are critically ill and they are not providing proper care inside the wards. The elderly are dying before their time due to a lack of care and this is happening on a regular basis inside NHS wards. Here is a quote from the Department of Health: "modern hospitals are providing high quality healthcare, which is safe and effective". Unfortunately we are being told lies because there are hundreds of "modern hospitals" where most of the wards are hazardous, vulnerable individuals are in danger, and there is a culture of medical negligence. The NHS are responsible for causing more than 1,200 unnecessary deaths every month inside the elderly wards, mental health wards, and the psychiatric wards and most of the victims are elderly. The true numbers of deaths due to negligence are much higher because there are a lot of incidents, which have not been reported and there are around 12,000 preventable deaths inside UK hospital wards every year caused by medical errors.

Some people may be familiar with the "Stafford Hospital Scandal". Thousands of victims died inside the hospital wards because they were ignored and neglected by doctors, nurses, and medical staff. In 2005, the higher managers decided to cut the hospital spending budget by cutting the staff numbers and doctors and nurses were forced to attend to the patients in the accident and emergency department in order to reach the new 4 hour waiting time targets. The higher managers were given financial rewards for reaching the NHS targets and they became obsessed with making sure that nobody had to wait for longer than 4 hours inside the A & E department without being seen. The doctors and nurses had to abandon people in the elderly wards in order to achieve the new targets. The staff levels were cut by 50% and the junior doctors were left in charge of individuals who were dying. The junior nurses switched off the heart monitors and life saving machines in the wards and they failed to monitor individuals with heart conditions. The elderly became distressed and dehydrated, while the doctors and nurses were busy attending to the patients in A & E. The nurses did not have enough time to feed the elderly and patients were left starving and hungry. Critically ill individuals were given the wrong medication and they were ignored by doctors, nurses, and healthcare workers. During 2005 to 2008, more than 1,200 victims passed away before their time. The elderly were abandoned by doctors and nurses who were put under too much pressure by the higher managers. The managers were guilty of a total failure of leadership and a lack of compassion and thousands of unfortunate victims were subjected to horrific cruelty and unnecessary suffering inside the wards in Stafford Hospital.

In 2002, a junior nurse from Southeast Asia moved to England and in 2009, he began work in a ward at Stepping Hill Hospital in Manchester. The managers and supervisors failed to notice anything unusual, but in reality the new staff member was spending a lot of time in the hospital dispensary where all the drugs are stored inside a huge cabinet. Unfortunately the nurse was hiding a dark secret inside and in 2011, he started to carry out his plan to murder people who were being admitted for treatment of minor health conditions that are easy to cure. Some of his intended victims died within hours of being admitted to his ward. He injected insulin into ampoules and bags containing saline solution, which are used for the rehydration of essential fluids within the physical body. The poison saline ampoules and poison saline bags were administered by staff members who were unaware of what was happening. The deceased individuals were suffering with health conditions, which are easy to treat and they were not seriously ill and they were expected to make a full recovery within a few days. The nurse continued to carry out his plan and there were 22 victims who lost their lives. In 2012, he was found guilty of 22 cases of murder and 34 cases of attempted murder and he was sentenced to life in prison. The unfortunate individuals who survived are still trying to recover from their injuries. NHS medical staff and the police were suspicious of the nurse's actions. Unfortunately hospital managers and chief executives refused to take any action and there is a lack of care inside a large number of local hospitals around the country.

St George's Hospital is in London and in 2009, a young man dialled 999 emergency, inside a hospital ward because he was experiencing extreme thirst and the nurses were not giving him any water. The man called the police and told them that the staff nurses were ignoring his requests for a drink and he had spent 48 hours without any water and he was feeling very ill. The hospital did not check an important letter sent by a GP informing them to make sure that the patient received his vital medication to control body fluid levels because the man had a condition, which causes "water retention". The doctors did not give the patient the vital medication and they did not check the fluid charts and the drug charts, which are used to keep a record of the patients medical treatment. The nurses failed to understand the concept of "water retention" and they thought that the patient was coming off recreational drugs. The healthcare professionals inside the ward failed to realize that a healthy young man was dying due to a lack of water and they dismissed the concerns of the police and the family. The patient was sedated by a consultant surgeon and the unfortunate individual passed away 12 hours later due to severe dehydration. The consultant doctor on duty failed to read the medical records and he failed to check the medical notes. The junior doctor dismissed the warnings given by a concerned family member and the coroner said that the death was caused by incompetence and medical negligence. St George's Hospital was responsible for causing the tragic death of a 22 year old UK citizen who went into hospital for a simple operation.

European Union working hours directives are limiting the amount of hours that doctors are allowed to work and this has created chaos within the NHS. Ignorant EU politicians in Brussels are responsible for causing a lot of suffering because they don't understand healthcare. Consultant doctors, junior doctors, and nurses are neglecting people who are seriously ill inside the elderly wards because they are being forced to attend to the new arrivals in the overcrowded accident and emergency departments in order to reach the 4 hour waiting time targets. Some managers have become obsessed with reaching targets and this has caused many thousands of premature deaths inside the hospital wards. The nurses and the junior doctors are overworked and they don't have enough time to provide any care in the elderly wards because they are too busy working in A & E. The locum doctors and the junior doctors are failing to diagnose and treat people correctly and they are carrying out pointless medical treatments and administering harmful drugs. The nurses are failing to notice the symptoms of side effects caused by toxic drugs drugs and they are ignoring important medical test results. The junior doctors are not being supervised properly because the consultant doctors are busy in A & E. Nurses and junior doctors are failing to carry out basic medical procedures and there are hundreds of medical errors inside local hospitals every hour, twenty four hours a day. There are four areas of basic healthcare. 1. Checking the blood pressure. 2. Checking the kidney function. 3. Checking the fluid replacement chart. 4. Checking the drug infusion chart. The nurses are not carrying out basic medical checks and the elderly are dying prematurely because the doctors have made too many unnecessary mistakes.

Hospital wards are too small and there is too much "noise" during the night time hours, which makes it difficult to sleep. The elderly are not receiving proper food and they are not drinking enough water. Large numbers of the elderly population are suffering due to dehydration and this is bad for the kidneys. Seriously ill elderly patients are being given unhealthy meals with large quantities of carbohydrates and cooked meat, which they can't eat because they are not able to swallow properly. Individuals with terminal respiratory infections are starving because they aren't being given any liquid nutrition and the nurses are unavailable. The consultant doctors, mental health clinicians, and the psychiatrists are administering medicines that cause injury and death and this is unacceptable. Elderly patients and mental health patients are being abandoned inside NHS wards. Psychiatric patients who are distressed and confused are being imprisoned inside disturbing surroundings and they are being forced to accept drugs and medical treatments that have no health benefits. Individuals who have psychosis are taking drugs that can cause permanent brain damage and paranoid delusions. Good quality care is based upon compassion and intuition and there is a lack of compassion and intuition within most local hospitals. The doctors and healthcare professionals are not telling people the whole truth. Many individuals are being given drugs and treatments that they don't need and this is a waste of money. When you have to visit a hospital ward to see a loved one who is being neglected and abused, it is just like torture. It is torture for the person who is being subjected to cruel treatment and medical procedures that cause injury and it is torture for the family who have to sit and watch a loved one who is suffering. When you have to leave your loved one in the evening, you are haunted by fear and when you come to visit your loved one in the morning, you are haunted by fear.

The human rights of vulnerable individuals are being violated by selfish greedy people who are dominating the system. We are living in a careless society and if you are rich, you can buy private hospital care, but if you are not rich, you are trapped inside the system. The elderly are being forced to die in public inside hospital wards where everyone can see everything that is happening. There should be a private room where the families and relatives can spend the last few hours with their loved ones in peace. There are thousands of families every year who have had their dignity taken away by the healthcare service because they have been denied the opportunity to take their loved ones home. Mental health patients and psychiatric patients are having their freedom taken away and they are being imprisoned inside NHS wards where they are not receiving any care or therapy. Most of the nurses have not been trained in mental healthcare and the clinicians and the psychiatrists are giving people poor quality drugs, which damage the central nervous system within the human brain. The elderly are developing bacterial infections that can cause the loss of life and there is a lack of dental care and skin care. The junior nurses are leaving metal canulas in the arms of patients causing them unnecessary pain and injury. The canula is a 2 inch long needle that the nurses insert into the patient's arm in order to administer fluid replacement, but within 24 hours the needle can cause uncomfortable pain because the nerves begin to send out pain reflex messages to the brain and the canula will need to be removed and inserted into a different place. The nurses are leaving the canula in the same place for too long and the elderly are having to endure the painful piercing of their arms and wrists.

Local hospitals are failing old people and young people. There is absence of urgency within most of the staff members and the system is too slow. Individuals with mental health diseases and psychiatric diseases are not being looked after by the private mental health providers and there is a total lack of psychiatric services. Medical professionals, consultant doctors, and GPs are guilty of ignorance and there is a lack of compassion within elderly healthcare, mental healthcare, and psychiatric healthcare. The medical staff are under extreme pressure and there is a culture of incompetence. Thousands of staff members have not been given the right training and they don't understand the needs of individuals who need therapy and healing. There are some wards that have managed to provide good quality care, but the majority of wards are not providing any care. People are being failed every day by doctors, nurses, clinicians, mental health staff, and psychiatric staff and there is a lack of respect. This is the "true reality" within NHS healthcare and when you have seen what happens inside an elderly ward, you will be shocked and disturbed. It is hard to forget the images of old people who had been "drugged up" and they didn't know what was going on around them. Can you imagine senior members of the royal family being subjected to this kind of neglect and abuse? It will never happen because we live in a fake society where the rich enjoy all of the privileges and the ordinary person is forced to accept poverty and poor quality treatment. The GPs are sending people to hospitals for tests and surgical procedures, which are painful and are not necessary and the consultant doctors and the junior doctors are administering harmful chemical substances. The NHS has got access to advanced technology and clinical knowledge, but in many cases, people are being mistreated and millions of UK citizens are being given poor quality treatment and expensive drugs that don't work. Elderly patients with terminal health conditions are being given deadly medicines that contain corrosive acids and this is against the law. 99% of UK doctors will refuse to admit that prescription medicines can cause the loss of life and they will continue to administer toxic drugs. The elderly population are being sent to a premature death and hospital nurses, mental health nurses, and psychiatric nurses are unaware of the symptoms of life threatening drug reactions. In reality there are many disturbing incidents that are happening every day inside the wards of horror.

10

CRISIS IN HEALTHCARE

You cannot deny the truth. The alarm bells are ringing because the system is not fit for purpose. There are too many rules and regulations that are not necessary. NHS healthcare managers and private social care providers are guilty of ignorance and arrogance and there are thousands of doctors, nurses, and care workers who have not been given proper training. Doctors and nurses are making too many basic errors and mistakes due to a lack of organisation and communication. Individuals with complex health problem are receiving poor quality hospital treatment and individuals with mental health conditions and psychiatric conditions are being given synthetic drugs that damage the vital functions within the central nervous system. Disabled people and young people with learning difficulties and attention deficit disorder are being ignored by the system and they are not receiving the help and assistance that they need. Individuals with disabilities and mental health conditions are being abused and mistreated by the staff members inside care homes, nursing homes, dementia homes, and disability homes. Most of the care workers and nurses are failing to provide any care because they are too busy and they are being overworked and underpaid. The social care industry is based upon a private ownership system, which receives money from the local authorities. If you can afford the cost of staying in a home, you will have to pay the provider around £50,000 a year for a single room and the residents have been used like a cash cow and they are being ripped off. If you can't afford the cost, you are totally dependent upon the government and increasing numbers of the elderly population are becoming homeless because the local authorities have had their spending levels cut by more than 50%.

The shortage of resources within the NHS is more than £30 billion and the chief executives are responsible for wasting millions of pounds every year. The powerful people who are controlling the system are not interested in providing therapy and healing and they don't understand the reality of human care needs. The directors of the pharmaceutical companies are dominating the healthcare industry and the prescription drug market is full of drugs that cause damage to the human brain and physical body. The media is busy talking about the 4 hour accident and emergency waiting time limits, but they are not talking about the large number of elderly patients who are passing away, while they are waiting on trolleys inside the busy hospital corridors. The wards are overcrowded and some of the corridors have become like emergency wards, there is a total lack of resources and a severe shortage of available beds. Critically ill individuals are having to wait inside the tiny corridors for more than 24 hours to get a bed in an elderly ward and there isn't any safeguarding in the wards during the night time hours. Some of the night nurses are aggressive and careless. The nurses are bullying distressed patients and this is disgraceful and totally unacceptable, as well as being illegal. You can't buy compassion and there is a lack of care inside hospitals across the UK. The national health service is full of foolish managers and chief executives who are full of vanity and self importance and there are many thousands of junior doctors, junior nurses, mental health staff, and psychiatric staff who have left the NHS because they were overworked and disillusioned.

Billions of pounds have been invested into healthcare and social care and the private companies have made billions in profits. The profits have not been invested into improving the standard of healthcare and social care because the money has been transferred into the secret bank accounts of global pharmaceutical drug companies, private companies, private social care providers, chief executives, and healthcare managers. Massive amounts of cash have been wasted and there are too many higher managers who are selfish and greedy. The higher managers at the top of the NHS are being paid too much money, the board of chief executives are incompetent, and the operational managers spend too much time having expensive business meetings inside their luxury offices. The elderly are suffering inside claustrophobic hospital wards and they are not receiving any care. Junior doctors and junior nurses are not trained properly and they are working in busy hospitals trying to help people, but in many cases, they are not fulfilling their duty of care. The elderly are in peril and there are fatal accidents taking place on daily basis inside hospitals and care homes due to the complete lack of proper safeguarding and there are more than 250,000 falls inside hospital wards every year. The total cost of elderly patient falls is £2.3 billion a year and most of the accidents are preventable. The elderly are being neglected during the night time hours and thousands of UK citizens have lost their lives because they had a fall. Falling over is one of the most common causes of death inside local hospitals and the hard stone floors are causing a problem. Polished hard stone floors are hazardous and if you are elderly and you hit your head or fracture your hip bone, the chances of death are very high. If you are a family member and your loved one has passed away because they had a fall in a hospital ward, it is a crisis.

A blind female patient died inside a local hospital in Sussex during 2017, because she was given toxic cleaning fluid by a nurse who thought that it was fruit juice. The orange coloured ajax cleaning fluid is used for cleaning the wards and the cleaner decided to pour the lethal liquid into a glass decanter, which is used for pouring water into the drinking glasses in the ward. The cleaner on duty left the decanter on a shelf next to the woman's bedside and you have to ask the question: why did the supervisors allow this to happen without intervening? The staff nurse on duty gave the orange liquid to the patient without checking or smelling the fluid because she thought it was orange juice and you have to ask the same question. There is a culture of ignorance within local hospitals and some of the staff members are guilty of negligence. The 85 year old victim died within hours after drinking the ajax fluid and her death could have been avoided if the staff members had been more careful and taken the time to check the contents of the glass decanter. The standard of care in hospitals and care homes is deteriorating and the government is not helping the situation. In 2004, the government introduced "new working hours limits" created by EU politicians and this had a bad effect on the quality of care inside the elderly wards. The doctors were overworked and the other doctors were not able to work the extra overtime in order to provide cover for the absent doctors. Consultant doctors and junior doctors were forced to abandon individuals who were critically ill because they were forced to work in the overcrowded accident and emergency departments. Hospital staff members who refused to follow "the orders" were dismissed immediately by higher managers who were ruthless.

In the cold winter of 2017-18, there were more than 34,000 deaths in four months due to influenza and every year there is a "flu crisis". An independent scientific medical report has found evidence that the flu vaccination is ineffective. Healthcare workers are not required to have the vaccine and there is a good reason for this. During the year of 2009-10, the GPs started to offer people the swine flu vaccine and NHS staff members were given the vaccination against their wishes. The name of the vaccine is Pandemrix and it was developed by a large private pharmaceutical drug company, the vaccine is harmful and it can cause narcolepsy, which is a sleeping illness. Hundreds of thousands of patients and hospital staff were given the Pandemrix vaccine and a lot of people were left with lifelong injuries and painful medical conditions. This is another example of the NHS creating a crisis because it is using artificial vaccines that don't work and cost millions of pounds. If a person is over 75 and their immune system is not working properly, an injection of toxic drugs contained in a vaccine will not solve the problem. If a person has developed type 2 diabetes and they are overweight, they will need an exercise plan/ weight loss plan. Synthetic drugs containing artificial chemicals will not solve the problem and there is an epidemic of type 2 diabetes spreading within the towns and cities.

The doctors and nurses are failing to look after the elderly and more than 70% of hospital beds are full up with patients who are over 75. We are living in a target driven culture where human beings are treated like "statistics", which can be manipulated to make sure the targets are reached. The British Nursing Agency (BNA) is making £50 million in profits every year and they are sending out hundreds of negligent nurses every day and vulnerable individuals are being abused by nurses who work for the BNA. UK doctors are causing the death of more than 1,000 elderly patients every month and there are many thousands of individual cases of "harm due to healthcare". The General Medical Council is destroying the criminal records of doctors who have a past history of misconduct and negligence. Many foreign doctors have not been given the correct training and individuals are being treated with a lack of respect. The government is refusing to accept the repeated warnings from the British Red Cross. Hundreds of hospitals are facing a humanitarian crisis in elderly healthcare and there are more than 30,000 UK pensioners who are trapped inside elderly wards. There is a total lack of social care and the funding system is not fit for purpose. The higher managers who run the NHS are receiving huge salaries and they are taking all of the profits, while many people are receiving poor quality care. The wards are full of chaos and there is absence of intelligent leadership.

Social services are not getting the funding that they need and there are big problems within local authorities. The elderly healthcare crisis is being created by the closure of thousands of care homes, nursing homes, dementia homes, disability homes, and specialist homes. The care industry has got a deficit of £1.5 billion and most of the providers are overcharging the residents because they have massive debts, there are a lot of financial problems within the industry and in 2017, an investigation carried out by the Care Quality Commission revealed evidence of a deteriorating standard of quality across the nation. The managers are spending more than £1,000 a night hiring agency nurses, the cost of living is rising and there are record levels of inflation. Local councils have run out of money and they cannot afford the cost of looking after the elderly, there are thousands of residential care homes where old people are being neglected and the government is failing the elderly population. The hedge fund managers of the private business companies are controlling the social care sector and the foreign owners who run the offshore companies are taking all of the profits. Local authorities are paying the care providers £330 a week, unfortunately the providers charge around £800 to £1,000 a week for each resident. Thousands of residents are being forced to sell their houses every year to pay the cost of social care and in many cases, they are being ignored and mistreated. In reality the big providers who are dominating social care are failing to look after thousands of residents every day, the big providers have got enormous debts and the independent UK regulators have found evidence of widespread abuse within residential homes and there were around 4,000 inspections into residential care homes carried out in 2017, and only 1 out of 400 dementia homes received an outstanding review. More than 60% of private residential care homes are not looking after people properly and they are providing poor quality social care. Large numbers of expensive specialist dementia homes are unsafe and the staff members are hostile, as well as being anti-social towards the residents.

Mental health patients and psychiatric patients have been failed by the system and many people end up inside a prison cell in a police station. More than 3,500 innocent individuals are being locked up inside mental health wards and psychiatric wards and young people with mental health conditions are being mistreated. More than 86 UK males will commit suicide every week and there is a lot of desperation in the towns and cities. Individuals are being subjected to physical violence and abuse inside psychiatric hospitals and they are being forcibly injected with drugs that cause disturbing hallucinations and paranoid delusions. The staff members have not been given enough training and they don't understand psychosis, schizophrenia, asperger's syndrome, autism, depression, thought disorders, panic attacks, and anxiety. The nurses don't understand toxicology and they are administering toxic drugs and there are hundreds of needless fatalities every year because the symptoms of the fatal side effects are being ignored by the staff. In reality the same mistakes are being repeated day after day inside mental health wards and psychiatric wards. Mistakes and errors can lead to a situation where a "disturbed person" has decided to kill a member of staff or another patient and during the period between 1993 to 2009, there were more than 900 murders inside mental health hospitals and psychiatric hospitals. This is a tragedy for the families of the victims, as well as the perpetrators, who are trapped inside a cycle of abuse and violence. Thousands of UK citizens end up having a mental health crisis because they are having to wait for many months in order to get a diagnosis and when they finally receive medical treatment, they are being given unnecessary injections of noxious chemicals, instead of therapy. Mental health staff and psychiatric staff are overworked and during an independent survey,

80% of mental health nurses say they are not able to provide any care and the patients are being neglected.

NHS hospitals have cut their costs to achieve the targets set by the government in order to become a foundation hospital, so that they can receive more money. Local hospitals with "foundation status" receive large financial rewards to improve the quality of care, but in reality many patients are trapped in disturbing surroundings. Old people are suffering because the higher managers are forcing the medical staff to abandon the elderly who are over 75 in order to protect their "foundation status". When you are with a sick family member inside a hospital ward, you will have to find a way to breakdown the brick wall. The system is the brick wall and there is a lack of honesty within the NHS. Consultant doctors, mental health clinicians, psychiatrists, and healthcare professionals will hide behind the wall if they think they have made an error of judgement and the managers are allowing this to happen on a daily basis. Hospital doctors and GPs have got an enormous amount of clinical knowledge, as well as access to advanced technology, but in reality they are unaware of hepatotoxicity and neurotoxicity caused by toxic prescription drugs. There are a lot of doctors who are guilty of a lack of understanding regarding the complex conditions that the elderly suffer from. The time has come for people to rise up and take down the wall because the politicians and civil servants are trying to stop positive change, which is a vital process within evolution and we need to start a peaceful global revolution.

Millions of workers in the UK are living and working in an unhealthy environment surrounded by pollution every day and they are also living an unhealthy lifestyle and they are eating too much fast food, drinking too much, and smoking too much. Children are becoming addicted to junk food and sugary drinks, as well as tobacco and alcohol. The soft drink companies and the global food companies are making billions in profits. The general public are consuming poor quality foods containing high levels of saturated fat, salt, and sugar, which is responsible for a large number of diseases. The future of modern hospitals will be based upon the use of powerful natural medicines that prevent illness and sickness. Independent medicine and independent science has moved forward and it has advanced over the last 50 years, but the national health service has not advanced at the same speed. If we accept that we are supposed to be living in a modern country with an advanced national health service, we are living in a fantasy world. People are voting for a service, which doesn't care about human beings because the system is being run by computers! The global drug industry is producing thousands of unsafe drugs and the NHS is responsible for causing thousands of serious injuries to the human brain and physical body every year. Cancer patients are being subjected to chemotherapy and radiotherapy treatment in order to destroy the malignant cells. These treatments are harmful and they damage the immune system. Some doctors and scientists have developed new immunotherapy treatments for cancer and new medicines to strengthen the immune system, instead of using noxious chemicals and harmful x-rays. Prevention is the key to wellbeing and millions of UK citizens are not eating sensibly and this is creating an obesity epidemic within our consumer society and will cost billions of pounds. There is new evidence to show that commercially grown wheat and white bread both contain tiny amounts of vital protein and they are full of large amounts of "artificial bulk", which is responsible for causing food intolerance and type 2 diabetes. UK citizens are working too many stressful hours where they are sat down without moving and this is having a bad effect on the blood circulation and the heart. We need to develop a new independent health system and a new independent social system based upon intuition and wisdom. Truth is medicine and there is no need for this crisis in healthcare.

EPILOGUE

The healthcare system and social care system are full of serious problems and we need to find new solutions in order to discover the sources of illness and sickness. The NHS is in crisis, the social care sector is collapsing, and the pharmaceutical industry is producing harmful toxic drugs.

The serious problems within the healthcare system and social care system are due to a lack of understanding and a lack of respect for the human body, mind, and spirit. The sources of illness and sickness are unhealthy lifestyles, environments full of pollution, fast food and junk food, deadly chemicals, harmful medical treatment, and dogmatic attitudes, which are against positive change. A simple solution will be found when evolution and revolution are allowed to happen within the medical establishment. New drug treatments and new medical treatments will be developed and people will be able to have access to good quality hospital care and social care. There are two very different worlds within society in the UK. Inside the happy world the person has received life saving treatment, which has increased their lifespan. This is a powerful experience and sometimes the NHS does wonderful work. Inside the sad world the person has received poor quality treatment, which has reduced their lifespan. This is a traumatic experience and sometimes the NHS makes unnecessary mistakes due to ignorance. When your life is in jeopardy, you have to be able to tell the difference between a friend and an enemy because they both wear the same clothes. We need new investment into the study of the physical body in order to unlock the secrets of medicine and health. We can find a cure for ignorance because knowledge is power.

AFTERWORD

Man made antibiotics contain substances capable of destroying or injuring living organisms, especially bacteria. Anti-depressant, anti-psychotic, anti-leptic, and anti-inflammatory should be written with a hyphen because they don't exist in nature and they should not be joined together.

The large drug companies are selling a fake product and in the majority of cases, individuals with mental health conditions and psychiatric conditions are being given noxious chemicals that damage the central nervous system. These chemicals are not "medicines". They are poisons and this is not "medication". It is reckless because there is evidence, which cannot be denied proving the link between toxic chemicals and permanent brain damage caused by the destruction of brain cells. The "functioning democracy" and the "free and fair" society are an illusion. The pharmaceutical industry is responsible for creating the antibiotic resistance crisis and they don't care about the ordinary person who lives in a village or town or a city. The politicians within the conservative government are acting like a group of "power obsessed puppets" in smart suits who are being controlled by the large global multinational corporations and this is not conspiracy theory, this is reality. Commercial industry is releasing poisons into the air, land, and sea. The drug companies have contaminated and corrupted nearly all of our natural medicines apart from a small group of "key medicines" that can cure illness and sickness. You cannot change the laws of the universe and there is a much safer way of treating people who are sick. Hippocrates is widely regarded as "the ancient father of modern medicine" and this was his philosophy: "let thy medicine do no harm".

REFERENCES

Independent Medical Sources UK

1. *NHS England.co.uk*
2. *National Office Of Statistics.co.uk*
3. *The Guardian.co.uk*
4. *The Times.co.uk*
5. *The Telegraph.co.uk*

Independent Medical Sources USA

1. *Dr Raymond Singer.com*
2. *Neurotox.com*
3. *Medscape.com*

www.ingramcontent.com/pod-product-compliance
Lightning Source LLC
Chambersburg PA
CBHW050417290526
45786CB00003B/1303